To Brigitta,
To my wonderful friend, classy lady as per person. This is the first & I'm so happy that I've signed you.

Judilee's Jubilee

With love & joy,
Judilee 😊

P.S. I'll call & set a date to come to my house for a tea-party as lunch. (I'll ask Joan, too!)

Judilee's Jubilee

A Memoir

*(the truth, the whole truth and nothing but the truth.
Well, that is, as far as I can remember...)*

Judilee C. Bennyhoff

AuthorHouse™
1663 Liberty Drive
Bloomington, IN 47403
www.authorhouse.com
Phone: 1-800-839-8640

© 2013 Judilee C. Bennyhoff. All rights reserved.

No part of this book may be reproduced, stored in a retrieval system, or transmitted by any means without the written permission of the author.

Published by AuthorHouse 4/12/2013

ISBN: 978-1-4817-3350-2 (sc)
ISBN: 978-1-4817-3349-6 (hc)
ISBN: 978-1-4817-3351-9 (e)

Library of Congress Control Number: 2013906418

Any people depicted in stock imagery provided by Thinkstock are models, and such images are being used for illustrative purposes only.

Certain stock imagery © Thinkstock.

Because of the dynamic nature of the Internet, any web addresses or links contained in this book may have changed since publication and may no longer be valid. The views expressed in this work are solely those of the author and do not necessarily reflect the views of the publisher, and the publisher hereby disclaims any responsibility for them.

Acknowledgement

Ah, Thank You...Thank You...

A big thank you goes out to our beautiful granddaughter, Sophia Alexander Orr. Sophie is 16 and the book that is now in your hands was typed by her—every single word. And I bet Sophie typed each chapter at least three, four... sometimes even five times. Not only that, Sophie had to read my longhand—a flowery curly- Q-ish cursive. Hey, that's not easy. Actually, in the beginning, Sophie would take a picture of a word and send it to my iPhone and say, "What's this word Doodie?"

You did a wonderful job, Sophie, you really did. You get an A+ and a gold star. And I thank you sooo much. We had fun, didn't we.

I love you, Sophie
Doodie/Judilee ☺

Dedication

My Memoir is Dedicated To ...

...George R. Bennyhoff, my wonderful husband and best friend extraordinaire. You take such good care of me. You are the best, you really are!

...Paul and Louise Cronrath, my loving, caring, kind parents. (Mother is now 97 years young)

...Last but not least, to our fantastic blended family...

> Jennifer Traynor Kostrubanic and Jim: Jaden, Evan, Layne, and Paige
>
> Gregory P. Traynor and Gwen: Connor, Logan, and Tyler
>
> Jodi Bennyhoff Orr and John: Mackenzie, Sophia, Priscilla, Charlie, and Henry
>
> Donald G. Bennyhoff and Kristin: Blake, Jordan, Morgan and Jack
>
> Dale G. Bennyhoff and Nicole: Haley, Gage and Zack

I love you all. I really do.

Judilee/Mom/Doodie XOXO

P.S. This book is the truth, the whole truth, and nothing but the truth – well, as far as I can remember. It was written just for you. You know, the punctuation isn't always where it should be and the grammar may not be particularly up to snuff either, but I said to myself – myself, ah forgetaboutit. My heart and soul are in these words, and to me that's much more important than perfect punctuation!

Preface

So Why Write a Book?

Our grandchildren started asking me...

"Doodie (like in Judie—that's what you all call me), "Is it true you had buck teeth like Sponge Bob Square Pants or Mater, from the movie CARS?"

"What was it like to live above a funeral home—were you scared?"

"Were you a model in New York City and you fell down—did you hurt yourself?"

Soooo I decided to write a little book or memoir (*Memoir; a record of events based on a writer's personal experiences*).

I had a dickens of a time coming up with just the right title—any title—I needed help here. So what to do?

GO TO GOD.

OK God, it's me Judilee, could you please help me find just the right title for my little book? (I don't usually ever ask for requests for myself, but this time I did.) Now some of you know I personally have a quiet faith in the guidance from above. Also, I believe that family and friends in heaven are looking out for me down here. This I know is true.

In exactly one week I had a name for my book and here's how that unfolded—to me they were signs from above. You might think this is corny but it works for me.

And here are my signs...

- My then 95 year old mother suggested, "Just call it Judilee. I liked what your daddy and I named you. It's a nice name too, different. Maybe you can put something with your name for the title of your little book."

- I was at a luncheon and my name tag read: Jubilee. The calligrapher, Judy Mileto, later apologized and said, "My sister has a farm called Jubilee and I automatically wrote Jubilee instead of Judilee. So sorry."

- My manicurist asked me what my name is—Judilee. Oh, said Joanne, "Your name is like Jubilee and that's the name of my church."

Do you see a pattern here?

- I had lunch at Nudy's with Barrie Jones (her husband's name is Barry too). She said, "Judilee I'll have to scoot soon—I have a board meeting for an organization called Jubilee. Isn't that neat?"

- My Town and Country, Vanity Fair, House Beautiful, and Oprah magazines arrived—all with the name Jubilee Bennyhoff— not Judilee Bennyhoff.

...Ah, that's it! Thank you GOD. *Jubilee, rejoicing, jubilation, celebration*—I'm celebrating a wonderful life so I'll name my memoir

Jubilee … Judilee. Actually, George suggested naming my memoir Judilee's Jubilee—and that's just what I'll do. Thank you, Honey!

And the color for the cover? That was a no brainer— Raspberry or hot pink—it's my favorite color.

Here is a sampling of suggestions for the title of my little book—

- So Who's Doodie (Nicole Bennyhoff)
- The Nine Lives of Judy the Kid (Jennifer Kostrubanic)
- Pizzazz (Bobbie Fanelle)
- Shit Happens (Jordan Bennyhoff, 17)
- Dancing on the Beach (Connor Traynor age, 7)
- The Unsnob Main Line Queen (Carol B. Aberdeen— she says, "The B stands for Bitch!" Carol keeps our home sparkling)
- It all started with a Coke Float (Priscilla Orr, 14)
- So Why Do You Wear So Many Accessories? (Jack Bennyhoff, 11)
- It's the Little Things In Life (Jaden Kostrubanic, 18)
- And She Lived Above the Funeral Home (Ginny Riley)
- Judi—isms (Kristin Bennyhoff)
- Shocking Pink and Velvet Black. (Leaugeay Phillips Weber) "Shocking pink for artistic, colorful Judilee and velvet black for funerals and sadness."
- Judilee's Spectacular Life (Paige Kostrubanic, 12)

- She Sparkles (Marianne McClennen)

- Eat Your Heart Out (Layne Kostrubanic, 13) "You always say that Doodie".

- The Crazy Wonderful Life of Judilee (Sophie Orr, 16)

Upstairs, Downstairs at the Funeral Home

I lived above a funeral home all my life. Paul E. Cronrath Funeral Home in Watsontown, Pa. My daddy was the funeral director. *(Funeral home; an establishment where the dead are prepared for burial and where funeral services are often held.)*

Daddy was a conscientious and compassionate funeral director. He said, "You know, Judilee, people don't usually die between the hours of 9-5. We're called out at all hours of the day and night and in all kinds of weather to remove a loved one. And a full moon always brings a lot of calls too for some reason."

<u>Downstairs</u> daddy had his office, parlor, storage room, cold room (where he kept flowers and sometimes cases of Coca-Cola and 7Up) and the preparation room where he prepared the deceased to be ready to be viewed.

Now people are always fascinated by daddy's profession. I'm asked the same question over and over - "so what does the preparation room look like and what does your dad do in there with those people?"

You know they want to know— but not really want to know— if you know what I mean! So if you're interested read on... if not, skip it.

Daddy's preparation room looks like a small, simple operating room. It has a morgue table with a silver crescent head rest at one end of the table. The morgue table tilts into a sink. There is a "Pulseator" machine which holds the embalming fluids. The Pulseator machine sits on top of a moveable metal table, which can then be moved next to the morgue table when needed. There's a tall white cabinet tucked in the corner that holds the varieties of embalming fluids. Did you know there are many different types of embalming fluids for your particular COD (cause of death)? Daddy used Dodge chemicals, the best, and the Dodge salesman would stop by the funeral home every few months. For years and years and years he came to call. His name was Harold Knapp - and we called him Knappie. Gee, he was a great man. Knappie always enjoyed a whiskey with daddy and many times he even stayed for dinner.

I'd heckle Knappie and say "paaaleeze , please please stay for dinner today...." I was a nuisance. He always told a good joke and I love telling a funny joke, too. I'd get so excited when I knew Knappie was coming to town. Knappie became one of daddy's best friends. A forever friend.

...Now where was I.... oh yes, now I remember, the prep' room... the bottles of embalming fluids are placed into the Pulseator machine. There is a ping-pong ball at the bottom of the Pulseator machine (honest, this is true...) When the machine is turned on, the ping-pong ball goes up and down and sounds like a heartbeat. BAH Bump BAH Bump Bah Bump....

Many times, when it was quiet at night and I was <u>upstairs</u> in bed, I'd hear the Pulseator machine, Bah bump Bah bump, and knew where daddy was in his procedure. Just a few more hours to go until he too, could come to bed.

Daddy's preparation room was neat and tidy. I think the walls were painted a soft blue. The room had a row of glass blocks to let the light in. There were no 'see through' windows - no one was ever going to peek at his "guests" - they were always respected and covered up with a clean sheet at all times.

Now that information may seem gross or perhaps freaky to some of you but remember, it's all I knew. You are what you know. Some dads are teachers, plumbers, doctors - my daddy happened to be a funeral director.

<u>Upstairs</u> were the living quarters for mother, my brother Gary, (who became a funeral director) daddy and I. Oh, and an Irish setter named, Pal. And she was my PAL.

While the funeral service was going on <u>downstairs</u> and we were <u>upstairs</u>, we could not walk around (no creaks) turn on the water or flush the toilet (no noise) or talk (which was particularly hard for me.) I had to sit right next to that big black phone and grab it on the very first ring, so the ringing couldn't be heard <u>downstairs</u> and you can imagine <u>upstairs</u> with our dog, Pal…eye yie yie, trying to keep a big dog content and quiet. So I rubbed her floppy red ears and hugged and kissed her during the funeral service.

I was sooo happy when the hearse and processional drove away. I could eat, talk, go to the bathroom and play with my dog, Pal, again.

Daddy gave me jobs to do—some were nice, some were not.

I did not like this job at all. I'm <u>downstairs</u> and I had to set up all those freaking folding chairs for the funeral. Yuck!

I hated that job. I would pout but it didn't get me anywhere. At all.

Daddy would say, "This will be a big funeral today, so set up all the chairs we have honey girl and try to keep the rows straight this time." Hey, that's like 50-60 chairs to set up. Or more. Whaaaa.

Now all those folding chairs were loaded and unloaded onto a moveable truck-thingy-on-wheels.

Still following? It held maybe a dozen chairs and it took all my strength—sometimes pushing with my butt to get that heavy load of chairs back into and out of the storage room.

Then after the funeral was over and all the people were gone, guess who put all these folding chairs back in the storage room? Yeah. Me.

Now there was one job I did like.

Well, sorta.

<u>Downstairs</u> I would remove every card from the flower arrangements and then write the giver's name into a pretty keep-sake book. The book was then given to the family.

The Kesslers; orange lilies, yellow fuji mums, delphiniums, asters. The Whites; a solid white arrangement of roses, snap dragons, stock, tulips, and baby's breath. Daddy was a detail person and he wanted me to identify the flowers and be specific as best I could. Not, blue flowers in a blue vase.

All righty then. Yes sir.

I got to identify numerous flowers with this job and I enjoyed it. And I guess it was one of my favorite jobs - I love flowers and love to write.

After the funeral was over, sometimes the family requested that some flower arrangements be delivered to the area churches or nursing homes. I was the driver and I received lots of smiles upon delivery of the flowers.

Oh, I just remembered something else people would ask me - "who would do the lady's hair when she's in the casket?"

Ouuu.

Mother did it.

Most beauticians did not like working on the deceased. Grace Wetten, a local beautician (who did Mother's hair for over 60 years), sometimes came to the funeral home. She carried a big wicker basket that had her hair supplies in it. Oh, sometimes my Aunt Marge, my fun red-headed aunt and also a beautician, would come and fluff and curl someone's hair. I liked when Aunt Marge came. I didn't do the hair. And you know why. Remember Dorie?! Oh, you haven't met Dorie, yet… she's in the next chapter.

That's not all…

Oh, gee, here's another question I was often asked. "What does a dead person feel like?" or I'd hear, "Ouuu, I get the hee.bee.jeebies… but, can I please go over and just touch her hand? Please. Please." (The deceased was in a casket, in the parlor, as daddy did not allow anyone in the preparation room. Period.)

"Go ahead… go touch her."

"Oooh-ooh—she's hard and cold." Well, whatever.

Now this job was not fun. It was a simpleton - mind numbing job. Remember when you go to a funeral home and you're handed a folded memorial card? The memorial cards come flat in a box and have to be folded. And you know who always folded those cards, don't you?

Me. The eedgit!

But daddy taught me a quick way to do it - take 6 cards at a time, fold them over once, crease heavily - and that speeds up the process. In other words, fold 6 at a time. Got it?

Just this year, I went to Dolly's house to fold note cards for the Devon Horse Show. Dolly said I was a lead folder, so there! And again that tip from Daddy came in handy.

George and I went to Boston for Greg's fundraiser for the Make a Wish Foundation. We offered to help Greg and Gwen do anything to get ready for their first big fundraiser.

…"Would you mind going to Staples and pick up the programs for Traynor Winter Classic and they'll be about 150 programs and they have to be folded?"

No problem – we're on it. Piece of cake!

George and I folded those babies in no time flat. Just in the nick of time before the fundraiser started.

Thanks Dad.

So keep that tip in your hat the next time you do your foldings. I always liked it when daddy would have a Catholic funeral. Know why? They usually had a mass card - no folding required. Hip Hip Hurray is what I'd say.

Oh, I almost forgot to tell you about the ribbons –

<u>Downstairs</u> after the funeral was over - many bouquets and hampers (*hamper; a large basket*) went to the cemetery to be placed on top of the grave. Each flower arrangement was always adorned with a huge big fluffy bow. And how I loved those big huge fluffy bows! The ribbons were at least 3" wide and the florist used yards and yards just to make one bow. The ribbons came in glorious colors - obviously, whites - then purples, pinks, blues, greens, and sometimes even gold or silver too. I was like a kid in a ribbon/trimmings shoppe. Daddy said I could remove every bow, but ONLY from the flowers going to the graveside, and I could keep the ribbons. OH boy, oh boy! …You

know those cheesy stick-on bows they sell now? I wouldn't be caught dead stickin one on my package - no siree - I'm a bow snob.

Yes I am.

And daddy got many hugs and kisses that day. He said, "The bows were a nuisance for the cemetery people and you might as well enjoy them, Judilee."

I was a happy girl. Yes indeedy.

Soooo I had my arms full of big bows, and I'd go <u>upstairs</u> to do-my-thing.

I would sit and undo the wire which held the ribbons together that made the big fluffy bows. I'd usually prick myself with the wire and my fingers always seem to sport a bandaid - but my efforts were well worth it.

Then I'd put up mother's ironing board and gently press each ribbon - being so careful not to scorch any. Next, I'd roll each freshly pressed ribbon and carefully attach a large paper clip to the end so the roll wouldn't unravel. I'd arrange the ribbons by color, and place them into a long narrow box. I kept the box under my bed and often pulled out my ribbon box and would rearrange the ribbons as I added new colors.

Say, this is sorta' pathetic!

I did use all my special ribbons to wrap gifts.

The gift receiver always gushed and said, "Oh, Judilee, I love how you've wrapped my gift—and such a gorgeous big bow."

So where do you buy your ribbons? I was NOT going to say, oh, I believe that one's from Mr. Mc Millen's funeral! Don't ever tell! Promise! Cross your heart and hope to die!

I was 12 or 13 at the time and this memory of downstairs at our funeral home might be sensitive but to me it taught me the essence of life…

It's about a little baby –

One of my great honors was to help daddy dress a darling baby girl. She was probably only a few months old and I don't remember her COD.

She was like a china doll. Daddy carefully put on her little white dress - I remember her dress had pink embroidered rose buds sprinkled across the collar. I gingerly put on her white booties with ruffles around the edge, a pink ribbon was woven thru the booties and I tied and retied it into the perfect little bow. Then next I put on her little white cap. Tears were running down my face and as I looked up at daddy I saw he was teary-eyed too. Then he put his arm around me and said, "You know, honeygirl, God needs all ages in heaven not just old people. God chooses special people; babies, children of all ages, teenagers. You have to have faith. This I know is true."

Daddy delicately placed that darling baby girl in a little white flocked casket. Then just as daddy and I were completing our final touches dressing that darling baby girl, the front door bell rang, and it was my good friend Marilyn Hile. Marilyn came into the parlor and we showed her the baby girl—one of God's little angels. Marilyn looked at the baby, then a big smile came across her face…(all the while I'm thinking what on Earth, why is Marilyn smiling.) Marilyn looked at us and said the baby's ruffle panties were put on backwards. Guess daddy didn't know that all those rows and rows of tiny white ruffles go in the back. He probably thought the ruffles looked nice in the front and I was still so upset, I didn't even notice. That moment sure broke the tension and the sadness we were all feeling. And now 50+ years later Marilyn and I are still talking and remembering that darling baby girl and her rows and rows of tiny little white ruffles.

Marilyn is another forever friend. She named her only daughter after her mother, Jeri, and me. Her name is Jerilee - isn't that a nice name. And Jerilee is as nice as her name.

I placed a small nosegay of sweet miniature pink roses and a cute brown teddy bear in the casket with her. Daddy's words stayed with me to this day. Have faith. We don't know when we'll be chosen, do we? I've seen all ages come and go <u>downstairs</u> at our funeral home- and it makes you appreciate every single day to the absolute fullest. Go for the brass ring, be in your life, show up for it.

Now on a lighter note - meanwhile, <u>upstairs</u> in the funeral home, my buddie, Carolyn Raup, whom I've known since I was 5 years old, came for a sleepover.

After we chitchatted and had our Coke floats—we went to bed and probably read Teen magazines or Photoplay. When I turned out the light I told her scary stories about "the guest" <u>downstairs</u>, Mrs. Casey, in the casket.

"Ahhhh, Mrs. Casey's sitting up, she is getting out of her casket now. She's folding her mauve velvet blanket and putting it back in her casket. She's stepping over the flowers...whoa, she got her foot caught in a big fluffy bow. She's stumbled - but she's OUT. And she's coming to get you, Carolyn. Mrs. Casey's still <u>downstairs</u> but she's turning the corner and starting to come <u>upstairs</u> now."

"First step."

"Second step."

"Ahhh, she's at the top of the staircase now. Mrs. Casey's slowly turning the corner and she's coming down the hall right to my bedroom."

"She's slowly opening my bedroom door."

"EEEEEEE"

"Here she comes, Carolyn. She's coming to get you. EEEEE…"

And to think Carolyn's still my good friend today!

Pigtails

Dorie was my next door neighbor. She lived right next door to our funeral home. We were about 5 or 6 then and when I was desperate, I'd have her come over to play.

She had freckles sprinkled across her nose, Dorie was so stinkin' cute.

I didn't like her.

AT ALL. And besides, she was bossy, always telling me what to do. She wore her silky blonde hair in long pigtails. She always had pretty ribbons tied to the ends of her pigtails.

Ah big deal.

Dorie looked like Goldilocks. Like I said, I didn't like her. I felt like I was the ugly duckling next to Dorie who resembled Cinderella. She was so darn adorable.

Whatever.

My hair was thin, mousey brown. Mother would give me one of those Tonette home perms (remember them?...they stunk). Well, of course you wouldn't remember those Tonette perms, you weren't even born yet. My memory is of sitting on a tall wobbly stool at our kitchen counter while mother rolled my hair in blue rods - rows and rows of rods - 'til my head felt top-heavy. Like a bobblehead. Then I'd hop off the wobbly stool, go to the sink, and mother would pour the cold perm solution all over my head. Ooooo, it stunk. It really did, I hated the smell of that Tonette perm solution. So here's what I'd do…I'd go grab a tissue, tear it in two, roll it up and then I'd stick the tissues up my nose to keep that stink out. And it worked. Picture two white tissue icicles hanging down from each nostril. Then I'd hop back on that wobbly stool and wait 15 minutes until the perm solution "took", or, let's just say, I would have curls once again. Mother never messed with my bangs, they were always kinda' crooked and straight. Hey, now you know why I love hats.

Now back to dear darling Dorie…

We played school teacher. Dorie was always the teacher who corrected my papers and I was always her student. We played candy shop and once again Dorie was the shopkeeper and I came to her shop with my pennies, to buy her stupid mud pies. Dorie was the nurse and I was her patient and she'd wrap my limbs in toilet paper (pretend gauze). Get it—Dorie was always the princess and I carried the crown (eerr, her crown which we made from weaving ivy, which grew on our brick funeral home). I woulda' loved to have used poison ivy for Dorie's crown.

Well guess what…this time we played beauty shop and I was the hairdresser.

Yes I was. I was so excited I could hardly stand it.

I hurriedly snuck into daddy's office and borrowed his gangly gold-handled scissors. I remember they were always on top of his desk in a long brown leather case - along with a mate—a long gold letter opener. (That letter opener always scared me - cripes, it was more like a small sword.)

So I grabbed those long scissors, with the gold handles, and went and got my little plastic purple comb and brush set. And then I was ready to open my beauty parlor. Well almost - I tied a tea towel around Dorie's neck and kept it closed with clothes pins. Just like a real beauty parlor.

AND I COULD HARDLY WAIT—to give Dorie a new "do".

Whoopie.

I grabbed Dorie's pigtails one at a time and hacked them off using those big gangly gold-handled scissors.

YES I DID! I remember it was hard hard cuttin' but I took them off right down to the nubs. That was the best 2 minutes of my life - hacking off Dorie's pigtails.

UH OH. But Dorie was so happy with her new hairdo. Her mother - not so much.

Dorie hated her pigtails and said she had to stand so still every morning while her mother pulled, tugged and braided her pigtails... those old fashioned rubber bands (not the colorful coated ones you have today) hurt so much and were always too tight. And then those silly ribbon bows tied on the end of each pigtail...Dorie didn't like them either. (But I liked her ribbons and bows - guess I was jealous. Well, ok, I was jealous of Dorie and her blonde pigtails with the pretty ribbons. Wouldn't you be?)

But her mother wasn't too happy with Dorie's hairdresser and I never ever had any more customers in my beauty shop! Never ever.

Oh phooey.

Buck Teeth

...Now my buckteeth looked like the old pick-em-up truck, Mater, in the movie CARS. Or perhaps Sponge Bob Square Pants' teeth come to mind.

They were that bad. And that's the truth.

Ask my mother.

When I was in bed at night, I couldn't close my lips because my teeth stuck out too far. Then my mouth would get so dry, like cotton, and I couldn't get to sleep. So here's what I'd do; I'd pull my bottom lip up over my buck teeth until I could close my mouth. Then I'd sleep on my stomach and that helped keep my mouth shut. And that's about the only time I kept my mouth shut.

When Judy Seebold and I were maybe 7 or 8 years old, we'd put on gymnastic shows for our mothers. They had to pay 15 cents (knowing me, back then I probably charged a buck!) for admission to our show. Then they got a hand-made ticket to come to our "Greatest Show on Earth". It took a long time to make our cheesy tickets and our show lasted only about 5 minutes. They got jipped.

Judy and I did our routine downstairs in the funeral home (no, we had no "guests" in the casket on the day of our performance). Besides, we had lots of room downstairs in the funeral home's parlor to sprawl out and do our fancy, dancey routines.

Our mothers sat on two folding chairs in the parlor and Judy collected the tickets. I, being the big-mouth, said, "Welcome one and all to Judy and Judilee's Greatest Show On Earth. Sit back, relax and enjoy our show".

Let the performance begin— get ready— get set—GO!

…I did a back bend, obviously with my mouth open, and, at the same time, Judy did a cartwheel. Somehow, with legs and arms flying, we got all tangled up— and my buck teeth got stuck in the heel of Judy's left foot.

Mrs. Seebold had to rush Judy to the emergency room where she had four or five stitches in her left heel – and a tetanus shot!. (*Tetanus; commonly called lockjaw, is caused by a bacterial toxin, or poison, that affects the nervous system.*)

Judy was hurting and I had loose teeth for days.

Boy, that surely was "The Greatest Show On Earth!"

Peeps

At Eastertime, when I was about 5 or 6, mother dressed me in a sweet new dress. I wore a straw hat that tied under my chin. It wasn't my favorite, but mother made me wear it and she said I looked so cute in it. I proudly wore black patent leather Mary Jane shoes and socks that had a ruffle around the edge. Did you ever wear those?

And off we went down to the Watsontown Park for an annual Easter egg hunt.

Each child was given a basket, with green straw at the bottom. Then we all lined up behind a rope. And then someone shouted – "ON YOUR MARK GET SET GO" – we all ran around like lunatics collecting colored eggs to put in our baskets.

Now some of the children received live, (and I really mean LIVE) cute, little, fluffy, peeps. (You know, baby chickens.) The peeps were dyed - there were pink peeps, green peeps, purple peeps, blue peeps and orange peeps. Nobody wanted the orange peeps - they looked sorta dirty-like. Poor things. Well, each child was given a box, probably a shoe box, and the box had little holes on the sides. And that's where we placed our peeps to take them home. Mine were the orange peeps. I felt sorry for them and nobody else wanted to take them home.

Hey, come on now, I know you've all gone to a fair and brought your gold fish home in a baggie. Yes, a baggie. Now fess up! So it's sorta' the same idea… peeps in a shoe box and gold fish in a baggie…

After the novelty wore off, I gave my orange peeps to my cousin, Sally. She, too, brought home peeps from the park. Her daddy eventually had to build her a chicken coop in their backyard – then Sally, later known as the chicken girl, bought a rooster.

Sometimes the chickens got loose in the neighborhood and the neighbors were scrambling around trying to catch Sally's chickens— and mine too. The chickens ran into everybody's backyard and up and down the alley. But that big rooster just puffed himself up and stayed right in that chicken coop waiting for his ladies to come home to roost. The rooster started his cockle-doodle-do-cockle-doodle-doing around dawn and drove all the neighbor's nuts.

My orange peeps found a really good home in the 'hen house' and I bet they lived happily ever after.

I named these peeps Eenie, Meenie, Mynie, and Moe.

Carrot and Bunny Wabbit Recital

Judy Seebold and I went to dancing classes at Mrs. Daley's School of Dance in Williamsport, Pa. We were probably 9 or 10 then. Judy and I carried little round patent leather cases with our tap shoes tucked inside, they zippered all the way around? We thought we were hot stuff. For our annual recital—our age group's dance routine was a barn yard theme with bunnies, carrots and a couple of trees. Some dancers were inside tall paper tree trunks—with holes cut out for their eyes. I did not want to be stuck inside any cardboard tree trunk, peeking out, or be in the very back row as a carrot.

No way.

The short dancers were bunnies and in the front row and the tall dancers were in the back row. Uh ha, Judy was tall and I was short. Guess who was in the front row?—in the very center of the row of bunnies? ME. Judy was in orange in the back row, a carrot.

My bunny costume was so elaborate. My big white fluffy ears were lined in pink satin – my headpiece tied under my chin. My furry bunny suit had a real fluffy round tail (like a powder puff) that flopped up and down. (And that's the only time I liked my butt floppin' up and down!)

And I still had the buck teeth to go with the bunny costume.

Well, after our barnyard dance routine was over, everybody left the stage.

Except me.

I kept on tap dancing and dancing…Alone. In the middle of the stage.

Mrs. Daley was behind the velvet curtain – on the sidelines – frantically waving her arms and motioning me to get off the stage.

NOW.

And I kept shaking my head and my big pink wobbly wabbit ears 'NO'. I refused to leave the stage.

WELLLL….

Mrs. Daley had to march right on stage and physically remove me.

I don't believe I was in any more dance recitals since then, but I still love to dance. Especially to the hit song, "SHOUT".

The Hearse

One summer evening Daddy was driving his gray 1958 Cadillac hearse (yes, with a casket in the back) through the town.

He came to a red light and naturally had to stop.

Now on the corner stood a bunch of rowdy guys, hooting and hollerin'..."hey mister, so who do you have in the back there?"

When the red light turned green- Daddy rolled down his window and without missing a beat he said, "well, I do believe it's your mother"...then he took off.

Daddy told me many times, "Do your thing, honeygirl. Be yourself and be generous to others…live your life and show up for it. Don't become possessed by your possessions. Because in all my years as a funeral director, I never ever saw a hearse pulling a U-HAUL".

Chewing Gum and Blowin' Bubbles

Well, when I was in 1st or 2nd grade I'm told I was a "pistol" (who knew).

I got caught chewing gum and blowing bubbles—in Miss Moser's class.

I could blow big ones, too, for my age. My buck teeth helped me get a good start on my bubble blowing. Remember, my teeth looked like Sponge Bob Square Pants' teeth. Maybe it was that huge gap between my front teeth but I blew great bubbles.

Yes I did.

My teacher, Miss Moser caught me blowin' a bubble. Miss Moser wasn't thrilled with me or my Double Bubble art form, or cracking my big wad of gum. Hey, do any of you chew? Or blow?

As my punishment for blowing bubbles, Miss Moser made me sit outside the classroom in the hall during recess. Uh Oh.

I can still remember sitting out there in the hall on that ugly little squeaky brown chair. The hall had a funny smell—like BO or sweaty socks—and all the kids knew why I was sitting out there, too.

PUN-ISHED.

Yep.

After recess, Miss Moser came out to the hall and told me to get back into her classroom.

I wouldn't budge.

"I like sittin' out here in the hall talking to my friends"…tra. la. la. la. la….

Miss Moser grabbed me by the arm and marched me right inside her classroom—ouch. And she made me sit in that crummy little squeaky brown chair right up front, right smack next to her big desk. Humph! Miss Moser was not my favorite teacher! Cripes and I'm only in 1st grade; do you think there's a pattern here?

Just a few months later, I was selected for May Queen. Go figure. Either Terry Keiser or Jerry Klapp was my King. I don't remember— both were cute dudes.

My wonderful mother and Grandma Bee made my dress. It was made out of cheese cloth. (*Cheese cloth, a lightweight cotton gauze of loose weave.*) The fabric scratched like hell— uh, excuse me, I meant to say, the fabric scratched like the dickens. I broke out in hives. That little dress had a ruffle around my neck and a ruffle at the hem and a green satin ribbon was tied at my waist. Mother made my crown out of white snowberries and ivy (which grew outside the preparation room). My little hand-held bouquet matched my crown and some of daddy's sweet pink roses were tucked in among the snowberries and ivy.

I didn't think I was very cute, but mother said, "You were cute to me". And that helped.

For May Day there was an elaborate Maypole dance and procession.

All the boys and girls carried colorful wide ribbons as they danced, circling round and round the May pole weaving their ribbons in and out.

And there I sat beside my king— with my crown sitting cockeyed over my crooked bangs and I was chewing gum and blowin' bubbles.

First Grade May Queen
8th Street School, Watsontown, Pennsylvania

P.S. Eat your heart out Dorie.

P.P.S. You, too, Miss Moser.

Pu-Pu-Pu-Err-L

I'll admit it; I can't say some words— like pearl comes out " PUHL", world "WUHD", oil "OLE" and Earl, like the guy's name, "OLE"… yeah, actually, it sounds just like oil.

Now you can just imagine how I pronounce squirrel.

In the good ol' days, back in the late 1950's, I drove a stick-shift Chevy (my daddy would say "Shivvy") Convertible.

And then I had to stop at a station for gas and oil (ole).

Uh Oh, this was always a challenge for me because remember I couldn't say that word. Ole.

So, I'd pull in to an Atlantic gas station— flash a big smile and say, "Hi, what's your name? Would you please filler' up with gas, check the water and please check the 'other'?"

Get it? Ah ha, I got by once again without saying that "oil" (ole) word.

And when I was in high school, I was a cheerleader and I could not pronounce the name of my school—Warrior Run (Woh-we-ah-wun).

It was pathetic.

Can you believe, after my divorce, I dated a guy named Earl (Ole). He never knew I couldn't say his name because I never said his name. Gee, he was such a nice guy too, but I had to give him the hook— so who wants to go out with a guy and you can't say his name?!

Wouldn't you know it our sons, Greg and Dale, both played baseball in Berwyn at Earl (Ole) field.

Man that was tough for me...

"What field are the boys playing at tonight?"

E-A-R-L Field.

"Ah, err, and my reply—Ole Field."

"Where?"

Hey, whatever!

But that's where I met George (Skipper)—Greg's team was playing against Dale's team at "Ole" Field!

YAY!

My future daughter- in-law, Gwen, spent an entire afternoon while we were in Baltimore to watch Greg play lacrosse at Ravens Stadium—we had hours to kill before the lacrosse game, sooooo Gwen helped me pronounce pearl. Just ask her— she worked with me for hours— I probably drove George and Gwen nuts. You know and I know I did.

I am both happy and proud to tell you that I can say it very, very slowly, but correctly— PA-PA-PA-ERR-L... just ask me to say it sometime!

There are many more words that I cannot pronounce but I'll never tell and you may never find out!! I sure hope not.

White, Padded, Quilted, Cone Bra

I was a late bloomer, really late getting my boobs (breasts). My bra looked exactly like the paper cup one gets at the water cooler. You know those small triangle cups sorta' looks like a teepee shape? ...now you can visualize that, can't you? Two cups side by side with straps = my bra.

Get the point?!

My quilted white bra was heavily padded. The cups were always standin' at full attention.

Let's fast forward a wee bit—

...Brucie Zettlemoyer asked me to go steady and if I'd like to wear his small gold basketball charm that was on a chain around his neck. (In the late 1950's, that was a cool thing to do.)

I said, "OH-Yes Brucie." So he put his basketball necklace around my neck and… and… well, we must have had a big, really big bear hug and Brucie squeezed me so tight with all his might. Uh oh guess what happened?

My bra cups became indented, concave like, and THEY STAYED IN THAT WAY.

Brucie looked down at my chest and said, "My oh my, …eye yie yie yie yie…yie…

I said not to worry, Brucie. Watch this—

And I pressed both arms next to my chest and then out popped my padded cups – back to full attention!

Lady Gaga eat your heart out.

Fly the Friendly Skies

A long time ago, I dreamed of becoming an airline hostess (stewardess). I wanted to fly the friendly skies and travel the world. And I wanted that job in the worst way - I wanted it so bad, I could taste it.

I'd wear the blue uniform, or a 2 piece suit with a short skirt. That blue suit would be paired with a matching blue hat that was the cat's meow - besides I never met a hat I didn't like.

Being an airline hostess had absolutely everything I loved…I'm a people person and all those flights had passengers coming and going. I'd meet-and-greet them and welcome them onboard. When passengers boarded Pan Am, the hostess (that'd be me) would pass out magazines and even offer blue decks of cards with the Pan Am logo on the front of each card. What could be better than that, giving gifts?

When children boarded the plane I'd lean down low to welcome them and pass out crayons and coloring books. The children were also given a pair of plastic pilot's wings… just like the one that'd be pinned on my blue uniform, only my wings wouldn't be plastic. They'd be the real deal.

Then serving the meals - sorta' like being a waitress. Hey, I worked summers at the College Grill and the Chatterbox in Ocean City, N.J. so that'd be a piece-of-cake. Coffee, tea, or me? I hoped they'd picked me.

Geez, I was so excited with the prospects of flying the friendly skies that even back then, I probably had heart palpations and was beside myself with wild anticipation and joy. Now remember, it was over 45 years ago and I'm trying to remember how I met most of the requirements to become a Pan Am hostess. I think you had to be at least 5'4" tall - perhaps wear a small size in a Pan Am uniform (I'm trying to be tactful here - no fatsos need apply). Perhaps one had to have a pleasant and pleasing personality and I'd try to do my best in that department.

I do remember taking a test that was given by the airline. Luckily I passed that test. But do you know what I didn't pass? I DID NOT pass my eye exam. An airline hostess back then was not allowed to wear glasses or even contact lenses. Maybe in the case of an emergency, if a hostess broke her glasses or her hard contact lenses popped out, the passengers would be, as my daddy said, " shit-outa'-luck". I guess I never got the memo about not wearing glasses or contacts.

But I do know I was crushed, devastated and I cried myself to sleep many nights. My dream of flying the friendly skies didn't work out for me. So, in life grandchildren, if you have a crushing disappointment, as Sinatra says, just pick yourself up, dust yourself off, and start all over again!

You will eventually find the perfect opportunity for you and then you, too, will be flyin' high....

The Black One-Arm, One-Piece, Swimsuit

Here's a little story that's embarrassing—but this is MY memoir, so please keep in mind it was ages ago and I was a teenager back then. Yes, I was a teenager once!

One summer I was a waitress at the College Grill on the boardwalk in Ocean City, New Jersey. It was THEE place to work, and it was near Bob's Grill, which was also a hip-happenin' place. I was never so happy to serve a hamburger and a Coke in all my life. The uniforms weren't bad either.

There was a waitress who worked there, too, called Bobbie (Roberta) and she had incredible boobs. And they were ALL hers. I know 'cuz I saw them myself. I couldn't believe it. If Bobbie pulled up her bra straps high—why she could choke herself. She needed a wheelbarrow to lug these things around. I bet Bobbie's cleavage (*cleavage; the act of splitting or dividing*) probably went down to her belly-button. And this is no B.S. Shameful.

Ooo, the guys were googlee-eyed over her. They all went crazy over Bobbie. It was hard not to like her—she really was a sweet girl—she never acted hoity-toity either. All the waitresses were so jealous of Bobbie—that goes for me too.

Meanwhile, back at our guest house on Wesley Avenue, some girlfriends and I rented a large room for the summer season. (Like six girls in a one room kinda' place). Maybe it was called The Sheldon Guest House—but then again, maybe I got that wrong—oh, whatever who cares. It was my day off and we were all going to go to the beach—the beach in front of the "grill". That's where all the cool guys hung out.

We shaved our legs, applied Coppertone suntan lotion, donned our best swimsuits, grabbed our sunglasses, beach towels and we're off to the beach. I wore my favorite swimsuit—it was a black one-arm, one-piece, swimsuit. It was very comfortable and not too revealing (like I had a lot to reveal—NOT). Today, you granddaughters wear itsy-bitsy bikinis and thongs...OH MY.

OH, Yes, I almost forgot the good part. Before we left the room—I hatched an idea. Hey girls what if we tucked those green wash clothes into our swimsuit bra cups—

we'd give Bobbie some competition.

"So, whaddya think?"

"Great idea, Judilee, YOU do it—we'll help you".

"OH, thanks! That'll make my boobs look bigger—nothing like Bobbie's boobs—but bigger for me."

We found two thin, cheesy, avocado green wash clothes and I tucked the wash clothes into my black one-arm, one-piece swimsuit. I was looking perky, if I do say so myself.

Now we're all off to the beach—walking on the boardwalk to get there. Fast.

Meanwhile, back on the beach, the guys were getting ready to play a game called Beach Blanket Bongo. So this is how that goes…the fellows would get a heavy blanket, like an old grey Army blanket—four guys would then grab each end of the blanket and make it taut (*Taut; tightly drawn*). Like a blanket toss. The guys would then go grab a girl—put her on top of the old Army blanket and toss her high to the sky. Up, up and away—(Remember the movie UP—wasn't that fun) high, higher and higher…

You know where I'm going with this don't you. Some guys started to run after me, uh oh, and I ran away as fast as my pedicured feet would take me. I ran in circles—then zigzagged around people who were trying to get some sun and read a book, I bumbled and stumbled across some little kids trying to build a sandcastle because—you know why…I DID NOT want to play Beach Blanket Bongo. (I know you're all on my side, rooting for me here).

By this time, the guys were closing in on me—"NO NO PLEASE"—I almost made it to the ocean's edge huffin' and puffin'. But my feet barely hit the water when they caught me from behind. Ah crap! And the more I carried on the more they wanted me on top of that Army blanket.

Soooo there I was ON TOP of that blanket being tossed UP, UP, AND AWAY. Lo' and behold—as I'm being tossed around—an edge of my cheesy green wash cloth was slowly peeking out from underneath my black one-arm, one-piece, swimsuit.

"Send Judilee higher, higher—high to the sky"—and with each toss a little bit more of the 'green' was starting to show.

Holy Crap.

Finally, I said to myself—myself—ah, what the heck, sooo I just reached in my black one-arm, one-piece, swimsuit and yanked out those green washcloths and then just threw them at the guys.

Whatever. (You know, I always wondered if the guys put a banana where it shouldn't be—or perhaps stick some washcloths 'down there' too! Hey I could loan you a few of my cheesy green ones.)

Later that sunny summer afternoon I was heading home—back to the guest house on Wesley Avenue. I was strolling on the boardwalk and bumped into a guy who was a grill cook at the College Grill. He said he was going my way and he'd walk the boards (boardwalk) with me. As usual I'm walking and talking and talking and walking—still in my black one-arm, one-piece, swimsuit—and I can't wait to ditch that suit. I certainly didn't have a spring to my step going home as I did going to the beach earlier—that's for sure.

As we were walking along minding our own "bidness" a man with a camera came up to us and asked if he could take our picture in front of the Ocean City Music Pier. He looked a little seedy, but we said, "OK, sure why not." The photographer took a few pictures of us. I made darn sure it was a frontal shot and not a side profile shot because now I wasn't so perky lookin'. Get me.

Just a few weeks later, there we were the two of us on the COVER of the Ocean City guide book (you know those freebee books that the Chamber of Commerce publishes).

The guide books hit the island around the same time that I had a date with a new guy. (I'll try and tie this together for you…) My new blind date, a friend of a friend, was going to pick me up at our Guest House around 7-ish. We were going to go to Somers Point to dance. Yes, maybe they'll play SHOUT. Hey, he had cool wheels (a car) Woo Hoo. It was a black Corvette with red interior. Double Woo Hoo.

But I've forgotten his name so let's call him Fred—or—Ted. Well let's call him Ted. Now the guys were not allowed in any rooms—they had to wait for their dates downstairs in the parlor (*Parlor; a room for receiving visitors; living room.*) This particular parlor was so fuggly— the walls wore drab wallpaper, like giant dusty-rose magnolias with huge leaves and vines—oooh ugly in every way. There were 2 settees (*settee, a long seat with a back and tufted tucks or buttons*). One settee was covered in a putrid mass of green velvet (*Putrid, in a state of foul decay or decomposition*). YES. That's the word I'm looking for here—putrid. The second settee had an equally awful fabric, maybe a reddish-rose color—thread bare too, there's more. The rug—oh geez—it reeked of cat pee, or not to show any partiality—it coulda' been dog pee, too. In the center of the room there was a huge oak round table—absolutely covered with newspapers, magazines, and the latest Ocean City guide book. The parlor looked like an old gramma's room. Funny thing, I can't remember my date's name, but I do remember that old musty smelling parlor. Go figure. Well, I can't figure...

When I bounced down the stairs to greet Fred (or was it Ted) well, Ted was standing in the parlor, right next to the big oak table and he was holding the current Ocean City guide book...the one with moi on the cover.

Ted looked at me, cocked his head, looked at the cover again and said...

"Haven't I seen you somewhere before?"

"Nah uh."

"I recognize that swimsuit. Are you sure I don't know you?"

"Nah, I don't think so." Phew. Hey, this room stinks—let's get outa' here."

"Oh, I do think I remember you now. Didn't you wear a black...

P.S. On the same day the Beach Blanket Bongo was taking place, mother and daddy decided to pay me a surprise visit. As they were walking on the boardwalk towards the College Grille, they saw a girl with long blonde hair being tossed in the air on the beach. Daddy said to mother, " I do believe that's our Judy there". Yep, it was me!

Glamour's Best Dressed College Girl Contest

I attended York Junior College (**YJC**) in York, Pennsylvania (now, it's York College). While there I dated a guy by the name of Guy Creep, who also lived above a funeral home, Creep's Funeral Home (isn't that creepy!). But we had lots in common and we talked about what it was like growing up living above a funeral home.

I was sad to hear that Guy Creep was killed in Vietnam, along with my handsome cousin, Mark Cronrath, but they'll never be forgotten. George (Skipper) and I visited the Vietnam Memorial in Washington, D.C. and we found their names inscribed on that long, black granite wall. Please, all of you go and pay your respects - the Vietnam Memorial is indescribable. (*Indescribable; too extraordinary for description*)

Well, back to **YJC**...

Some friends, actually two fellows in my math class, entered me in **GLAMOUR'S** 1961 "Ten Best Dressed College Girls" contest. The judging standards used by the magazine are:

1. Nice figure, beautiful posture

2. Good grooming - not just neat but impeccable

3. Appropriate collegiate look

4. Individuality in use of colors and accessories

5. Pleasing personality

According to the contest's description, "The ten winners will spend two glorious weeks wining and dining in New York City and will stay at the Biltmore Hotel. They will model everything from swimming suits to ball gowns and will be given the complete wardrobe that they model. The "Ten best dressed" will also be presented with a Remington Rand typewriter, perfumes from Lanvin and Dana, glamorous round of famous night clubs, and a dinner dance on a cruise boat on the Hudson River with the Yale Club." The Yale Club - oh, boy oh boy.

The Contestants were to send 3 photos of themselves in various outfits…one in a party dress, one in a collegiate outfit and I've forgotten the other category, maybe a bathing suit.

The final contestants (5,000 entered) were narrowed down to a few and moi was in that few.

Woo Hoo!

The kid who lived above the funeral home in a national contest… and…a finalist. Maybe even featured in Glamour magazine.

Hip hip hurray, it's gonna' be a good day.

On March 15, 1961, I received a WESTERN UNION telegram. Now I bet all you grandchildren, or for that matter our children, have never even seen a telegram or know what a telegram looks like. (*Telegram: a message sent by telegraph. Telegraph: A system or apparatus for transmitting messages over a distance by coded electrical signals sent by wire or radio; to transmit a message to a person.*)

And this is exactly what my telegram said:

> New York NY 15 420P EST=
> Miss Judilee Cronrath, York Junior College=
> 232 South Duke St. York Penn=
>
> Picture of your party dress has not yet arrived. We must receive it by beginning of next week=
>
> Lucia Carpenter   Glamour College Contest.

I've saved my yellow paper telegram - as it's tangible (*Tangible: Capable of being touched... Real or actual*). Soooo come on over and I'll show it to you - it's in my portfolio. (I know what you're thinking, geez, she's old!) Yeah, you're right!

Let's get back to "Glamour's Best Dressed College Girls" contest...

People in my hometown of Watsontown, Pa. were all cheering for the hometown girl. And my friends at York Junior College were rooting' 'en tooting' too. People would say things like "I just know you're going to win" or "it's in the bag"..."you'll win for sure - you just got that telegram"...

All those comments got me so fired-up and I was sooo excited with wild anticipation - and Hey, there just might be a chance here. I visualized two glorious weeks in New York City - staying at the Biltmore Hotel. Meeting new friends from other colleges. Oh yes, the cruise on the Hudson River with the Yale Club. YES! AB-SA-TOOT-LEE! I especially wanted that Lanvin perfume. It was a pretty bottle.

I thought my halo was about to pop up and twirl around, ah yes.

Well, I LOST.

BUM-MER.

A Miss Martha Kostyra, from Nutley, New Jersey won the contest.

My daddy said, "Hell, with a name like that honeygirl, you should have won the contest!"

And I'm still mad at Martha Stewart! Yeah, THAT Martha Stewart.

But I became a cheerleader at **YJC** and I bet Martha wasn't a cheerleader.

So there! (Sore loser)

P.S. Later, one of my friends found out that no Junior College applicants were considered because of the overwhelming number of contestants. Ah well, that made me feel a wee bit better. Well, not really.

Big Feet

When I was married the first time, my wedding slippers were size 7.

Then when I got married the second time, my wedding shoes were size 9. And now I wear a 10 (in cheap shoes maybe even a bigger size).

Go figure.

I don't have fallin' arches either. My feet just grew as I'm told my ears might grow, too, as one gets older.

Jean French, my dear petite friend, has tiny feet. 5 ½.

Ah, big deal.

Well, Jean can place her entire shoes inside my big shoes. And she does. Then she'll do a soft-shoe dance routine, laughing like a hyena.

You had to be there!

Actually, Jean's skit was funny…and then I got to thinking… but, Jean, I get more bang-for- the- buck in shoe leather!

Judilee's Jubilee

SO Lah-dee-dah.

I'm really not a shoe person. Not at all actually. No Jimmy Choo's or Louboutin's in my closet.

But Georgie Porgie, he has at least 65 pairs of shoes. Now admit it, George, you know and I know that I'm right. The wife's always right. Happy wife—Happy life.

Now just last year, George and I went to the antique mall in Mullica Hill, New Jersey.

We always split up and meet an hour later at a designated place. He likes military memorabilia, antique guns and guy things. And I'm more into girly things – antique dolls, china, and jewelry.

After an hour, we met and George was soooo excited to see me.

AH, that was nice.

George had a big grin from ear to ear and said he'd found the perfect gift for me.

"You'll love it. Let's go downstairs and it's right under the staircase."

Oh, I could hardly wait. George was just so thrilled with himself. What could it be??

You know what was sittin' right there under that staircase?

A HUGE pair of yellow clown shoes. At least 24".

(And to think this is all true. Hey, I couldn't even make up this shit!)

New York, New York

You've asked me how I got to New York City—the Big Apple— well, here's that story…Once upon a time I attended Williamsport School of Commerce; learning how to become a medical secretary. I did well at school and after the courses were finished the Director called me into his office.

Uh-oh!

"Did I do something wrong?"

"No"

"Whew!"

The Director, at the school, wore special custom-made brown shoes— his left foot had a1" or 2" thick sole. He walked with a limp and had great difficulty maneuvering the steps. Perhaps he had a club foot or perhaps another deformity.

The students made fun of him—but I didn't—the director was one of the nicest, kindest men I've ever met. Besides daddy. And Georgie Porgie.

There I am sitting in the director's office. He said there was a possibility of a medical secretary position in New York City. The position was at the New York Hospital— Cornell Medical Center— Payne Whitney Psychiatric Clinic.

He asked if I would I be at all interested in the job?

Are you kidding?!

Absolutely! Having a chance to go to New York City to work—yes indeedy!

Mother and daddy drove me to New York City for my interview. They sat in the lobby, on a pair of plush moss green colored love seats placed in front of a fireplace at the Psychiatric Clinic. (I loved the color of those green love seats.)

The medical secretary position, at Payne Whitney Psychiatric Clinic, would be working exclusively for three psychiatrists. (*Psychiatry, the branch of medicine concerned with the study, diagnosis, and treatment of mental disorders.*)

Dr. Lewis interviewed me first. He gave me a tour of the clinic and explained the job requirements. Dr. Lewis asked me a lot of personal questions, and, you know, for some odd reason I wasn't the least bit nervous. (I tell it as it is and what will be, will be.)

Dr. Lewis showed me the office for the 'new girl'...

WOW! The office was posh. (*Posh; stylishly elegant, luxurious*)

The office was next to the Admitting Office and at the very end of the hall on the first floor of the clinic. One could look down the long corridor straight into the posh office (no nose picking here; one was on full display).

Then I met with Dr. Wainwright and Dr. Sharp.

Guess what?

I was hired on the spot.

WAHOO! I was over the moon.

I had to pinch myself (actually I went into the ladies room and danced all around the toilets—nobody saw me). The buck toothed, 4-eyed kid from Watsontown, Pa. who lived above the funeral home, was now working for three psychiatrists in New York City— at the world famous Payne Whitney Psychiatric Clinic.

Ha-low!!

And I was to start in one week. Now where to stay? I didn't know one single soul in New York City.

Not one person.

Somebody suggested the YWCA (Young Women's Christian Association) they might have a room to rent. And they did. And that's where I went.

Daddy's grey Cadillac sedan was in the shop for repairs so he had to take me to New York City in his Cadillac hearse. (*Hearse; a vehicle for conveying a dead person to the place of burial*)

Oh, if anybody saw me getting out of a hearse!

I had two suitcases and one alarm clock – my worldly possessions.

Daddy couldn't stay because he 'got a call' that morning and had to get right back to the funeral home— where mother was 'tending the shop.' And besides daddy had the hearse.

At the YWCA, men were not allowed in any of the rooms. Period. (Now wasn't that the good ol' days—no men in the rooms!)

Even though' I tried to sweet talk the old lady at the front desk to allow daddy to help me carry my two heavy suitcases to my room…

Sweet talkin' didn't work.

"Don't you know what 'No' means?" (Well at least I was tenacious—you old fart!)

I stood at the curb, a little tear running down my cheek, and I kissed and hugged daddy goodbye as he waved and drove away in his long grey Cadillac hearse. Then I lugged my two suitcases up to the 5th floor.

It was a humid Indian summer day in New York City. My room was small, it had two windows— with no A/C (unit was broken) the other window didn't open either – probably painted shut. But I did have a cute little fan in the room.

So once again, sweating like a little piglet, I set my alarm clock and tried to get a good- night's sleep. I wanted to be refreshed for my first day at the psychiatric clinic…

No sleep. Not at all. Too hot.

Nada.

Next morning, bleary eyed, I got dressed—wearing a boring but safe outfit I might add.

I went down to the front desk, the old fart was back!

I wasn't exactly sure which way to walk to work—Uptown, Downtown—Eastside, Westside? And I was not going to ask that grumpy old lady at the front desk.

Well, I made it to work; I was even early, for my first day at the Payne Whitney Psychiatric Clinic. I LOVED, loved my job.

…lets fast forward here…

Soon I met some neat girls and eventually we got an apartment together.

We four girls were stuffed into a small 1 bedroom apartment— 5th floor walkup— on the upper East side of New York City.

No door man here!

Ah, such fun we had and the stories I could tell. I could write a book just on our escapades. (*Escapade; a reckless adventure, shenanigans*)

Here's just one story...Our roommate, Ellen, had a boyfriend who was on Jacqueline Kennedy's Secret Service detail. Now you grandchildren all remember that Jacqueline Kennedy's husband was JFK— John Fitzgerald Kennedy— President of the United States of America 1961-1963. Ellen's boyfriend told us newsworthy events even before it hit the newspapers.

But what was never to be mentioned was— Mrs. Kennedy smoked cigarettes.

Newports.

Who knew?

She was never ever to be photographed holding or smoking a cigarette. Ellen's boyfriend also told us that "there was something funny about her fingers— she chewed her nails or supposedly had club-like fingers" (Now what does that mean—I dunno.) Once again Jackie Kennedy was never ever to be photographed showing her hands or smoking a cigarette. We all found that fascinating—as from the 1960s I don't believe I ever saw a photo of Jacqueline Kennedy showing her hands or smoking a cigarette. Mrs. Kennedy usually wore gloves; her hands were either tucked in her pockets or wrapped around a clutch bag.

Ellen's boyfriend said Mrs. Kennedy had a "soft funny voice— but she was so very nice to us Secret Service guys". He used to light her cigarettes and she liked that. In the White House you'd find cigarettes in sterling silver cigarette holders. An ashtray was placed in front of the holders. The presidential emblem was embossed on both pieces of sterling. You'd find cigarettes in most rooms of the White House. But back then most people smoked. I did. Newports, too.

By the way, guess how much a pack of cigarettes cost back then? 25 cents. Yes. I paid 25 cents for a pack of cigarettes. Now here's something else… if I bought my Newports from a cigarette machine they cost more. If I put three dimes into the machine, out popped a pack of cigarettes that had three pennies tucked inside the cellophane of the pack. Honest, this is true. Go ask your grandfather. Or your grandmother. Say, I always wondered who placed those pennies in each and every pack of cigarettes. Maybe elves?

Oh, and another comment Ellen's boyfriend told us about Mrs. Kennedy—she had big feet—just like mine. Mrs. Kennedy wore a size 10 ½ narrow—and now I'm a size 10. It's another reason why I admire her.

… I'd love to tell you more—but I won't—so let's get back to the psychiatric clinic.

At the Payne Whitney Psychiatric Clinic we had famous patients. Even Marilyn Monroe was a patient there— but that was before I went to work at the clinic. I'm told that her husband at the time, Joe DiMaggio' (a famous baseball player) came to see Marilyn every day and brought her a long stemmed red rose. We had movie stars, playwrights, poets, authors, artists, TV personalities and Broadway stars as patients—most were famous and recognizable.

It was soooo hard not to gawk and stare—I signed a confidentiality (*confidential; entrusted with private affairs*) paper with one of the doctors, the doctor who treated the famous—and stated that, in essence, I would not reveal any information or tales about his famous patients.

I gave my word and to this day I've kept my honor and integrity.

My lips are sealed.

But you wouldn't believe!

I so enjoyed working for Drs. Lewis, Wainwright and Sharp. The doctors were so kind to me. I did my best.

I would babysit for Dr. Lewis' sons and also for psych residents' children. The doctors were good tippers. And I needed the money. I also worked one night a week at Bloomingdales—in the hosiery (stocking) department—and later moved to bras and undergarments. I sure liked that department. There are some juicy stories from that lingerie (*lingerie; women's undergarments*) department as the men were purchasing delicate 'undergarments' for their girlfriends…err, wives.

Then I started dating the Chief Resident, Dr. Robert Daly— he was another great guy. Bob had a party, I was his hostess at the party and that's where I met my first husband-to-be. And you know the rest!

Here Comes the Bride

When I lived in New York City, I did some modeling. That was back loooong ago, when I was 5'6¼" and weighed a little over 100 lbs. Whoa! Now I'm lucky to be 5'4" and we will not discuss my weight.

And don't ask me either, because I won't tell you.

I was "booked" to model for a bridal fashion show at either B. Altman or Bergdorf Goodman (my memory is a little off, too), both fabulous stores on Fifth Avenue in New York City.

The Bridal fashion show was by invitation only—which meant limited seating to VIPs (Very Important Persons). I modeled some beautiful bridesmaids and bridal dresses. Some were nice—some not so nice. The fashion at that time was for long flowing bridal gowns with lots of lace appliqué *(applique; a cutout design of one material appliqued to another)*. Maybe, sorta' like a Cinderella gown—certainly not like the sleek and sexy bridal gowns of today.

I sashayed down the long runway in various bridesmaid dresses, pausing to look left and right at the audience. Some of the gowns I wore were hideous, but I always wore a smile, but was thinking, this is an awful lookin' frumpy rag I'm showing.

For the grand finale (*finale; the concluding part of something*), I was the bride, all wrapped in white lace, taffeta and tulle (*tulle; [pronounced "tool"] a thin, fine net of nylon, rayon or silk*). As I was approaching the end of the long runway—getting ready for my turn-about, suddenly I was having a problem with my contact lens. A reeeally big problem. Uh oh…OH NO…

Now perhaps I should pause here to tell you about my contact lenses. I'll be quick.

They were invented in the 1950's, my era, and I had one of the very first pair of contact lenses. The lenses were made of glass—hence, they were called hard lenses. Now to get use to wearing glass- in-my-eyes (literally), each day I'd wear my contacts for 1 hour…the next day for 2 hours…3rd day for 3 hours…etc…etc… and increase the times until I could try to wear my contacts all day long. By doing so, one's eye lids would become calloused. This process was very painful for me. But by this time I was getting tired of being called, "4 eyes" or "google-e eyes", but I persevered. Yes siree. I was determined.

Now here's a little game I played by myself.

To remove my hard contact lens, I'd pull on the corner of my right eye—and the hard lens would pop right out—hopefully landing smack into my cupped left hand. Then the left lens—landing into my right cupped hand. Hey, I was getting good for someone who's uncoordinated.

Why did I play that game by myself? Who knows! I don't.

Many times I missed my aim and there I'd be in the bathroom on my hands and knees. Since the little buggers would ricochet (*ricochet; the rebound of an object after it hits a surface*). I'd be lookin' for my contact lenses on the floor, on the vanity counter, in the sink, in the fluffy pink throw rug (one time I even found my lens inside the Kleenex box)…all the while thinking…WHERE ARE

YOU—YOU MISERABLE LITTLE THING? I know this is such a stupid game, and I'm playing all by myself. Ah, gee whiz.

Meanwhile, people were knocking on the bathroom door to get in to pee (we only had one bathroom).

Knock... Knock..."Judilee, what are you doing in there?" There I am still in the bathroom on my hands and knees lookin' all around for my contact lens. I think I told them I was on the John—it gave me more time for the hunt.

But the knocking on the bathroom door became louder and louder...

Knock...knock...knock..."open up"!

"OK. Come on in and watch where you're steppin'—I haven't found my contact yet. Pee fast. Puh-lease."

When I returned to the bathroom, I took 3 or 4 steps and stepped on something...

Oh no— BRO-KEN CON-TACT BUM-MER. Serves me right for playing that silly, stupid game.

One set of contact lenses had to last a long time—maybe even a year or until your next doctor's appointment when you'd get a new prescription. Not like today when you grandchildren sleep in your lenses—or dispose of them daily. Hey, that's wonderful.

And to this day I still have my original glass contact lenses. They're kept in a cute little blue snap case. Come on over and I'll show you sometime.

Oh, you granddaughters, it's not true that guys don't make passes at girls who wear glasses. Skipper makes passes at me and I'm back to wearing glasses! My glasses are invisible-like, rimless, and a very light "honeydew" color. When I take them off and put them down somewhere—which is all the time—I have to heckle Skipper into helping me find my "invisible" glasses. Sorta' like going back in time and lookin' for my hard contact lenses. Can you please help me find....hey, I'm pushing my luck here with Skipper!

See, I always get off the track and ramble on, so let's get back to the bridal fashion show—invitation only—for VIP's—in New York City, at B. Altman or Bergdorf Goodman. The more I think about it, I'm pretty sure the fashion show was at Bergdorf's.

Okay, now I'm in my beautiful appliqued bridal gown, at the end of the long runway—ah, poetry in motion—and I'm getting ready for my turn-about. I stooped down to gather up my train, trying to keep the veil out of my face, meanwhile holding onto a fake ugly looking bouquet—AND—suddenly for some reason, my eyes started to go nuts. My right hard lens popped right out of my eye, while my left lens went up in my eyeball. WAAAY up. Somewhere (I don't know where the heck it went, but I do know it was sooo painful). Then I began blinking and rolling and twitching my eyes like a lunatic—not to mention my facial expressions and gyrations. I was so discombobulated... swaying to and fro.... still at the very end of the runway, staggering around.

Feel for me here. Then the heel of my white satin wedding shoes got stuck in all that fluffy white tulle—then I lost my balance, fell off the end of the runway and landed right into the lap of a VIP guest. Front and center. Best-seats-kind-of-guest.

OMG

Actually I plopped smack into the lap of a father-of-the-bride. I wanted to burst out crying but my eyes were already red and sore and watering from my, um, shall we say little incident. That startled father-of-the-bride helped me put my white satin shoes back on, helped me get to my feet, and gave me a bear hug. Then he stood up and said, "Now this is some damn bridal show—let's give a big round of applause for this bride (moi)".

P.S. See that old timey picture of me in that wedding gown—that WAS the bridal dress and appliqued head piece that I modeled long ago in that bridal show in NYC. I was also wearing a long auburn wig and all that thick hair felt sooo good—I was flinging my fake hair all around (hey, my hair was almost as thick as Dorie's—remember her? I cut off her pigtails).

So that's my here comes the bride story. But a few chapters away, there's another here comes the bride story, only this time I AM the bride. For real. Yes I am. Yippee eye aye.

My Namesake—Judy Garland

Yes, it's true; I was named after Judy Garland (as in Dorothy from *The Wizard of Oz*).

She was a famous singer as well as an actress.

I was living in New York City when Judy Garland died. She died in Europe, was embalmed in Europe, and her body was flown back to New York City for her funeral. I was absolutely determined to see Judy Garland—see how she looked, see what she was wearing, check out the funeral home—and then relay every little detail back to mother and daddy.

If memory serves me, Judy's funeral was at Frank E. Campbell Funeral Home. The family announced that the funeral home doors would remain open all thru' the night until everybody had a chance to pay their respects to Judy Garland.

My husband at the time said, "Judilee, you are NOT going to see Judy Garland. It's after midnight and too late now—so give it up."

Hmmm, by now, you know and I know that I was going to see Judy Garland.

Soooo, I waited until he was sound asleep and snoring softly....

then, as quiet as a church mouse, I slowly got up out of bed and got myself dressed (in the dark). I even remember what I wore that night long ago—I wore a yellow linen dress with a matching coat and even sported a little straw hat with a sunflower plopped on the brim. I got all dolled-up to pay my respects to my namesake, Judy Garland.

Truthfully, I was a little bit scared to walk all alone, in the dark, late at night, in New York City, at around 1 or 2 AM. (like crap-my-pants kinda' scared.)

I grabbed a Time Magazine and rolled it around a pair of scissors—just in case I got mugged. (And why scissors and not a steak knife I'll never know.)

We lived at 83rd Street and Third Avenue and I think it was quite a long walk to the funeral home. I walked fast—a big spring to my step—and huffin' and puffin' to get there quick. I arrived at the funeral home and, you know, I was the very last person in the door. YAHOO! Made it.

I vividly remember being nervous, scared, and yet excited—and—also thinking what the hell am I doing here at this time of night.

So there I stood, the last person in the funeral home, standing at the end of a long aisle. What a sight it was. I just stood there taking it all in. And nobody rushed me which I appreciated.

My first impression was a huge, colorful "Over the Rainbow" flower tribute from Frank Sinatra. (Do you remember the colors of the rainbow? ROY G BIV- which means red, orange, yellow, green, blue, indigo and violet. Skipper taught me that—it's fun to know). The rainbow floral arrangement was arched, just like a rainbow, behind Judy Garland's casket. Judy Garland sang "Over the Rainbow" in the movie *The Wizard of OZ*. That song became her trademark song. There were such fabulous flower tributes—spectacular is the word

I'm looking for here—the likes of which I have never seen before and have never seen since. The sweet smells of all those flowers, ah, the heavenly scents.

I slowly walked down that long aisle, and there she was—JUDY GARLAND.

Judy Garland's casket was low to the ground – I was looking down at her—in full view—which actually startled me at first. I don't know how to describe this but there was a plastic, or a glass that completely covered her body so no one could reach down and touch her.

Judy Garland was tiny. She had short dark hair, and wore red-orange lipstick (like my bright orange dress which I'll tell about later). And it seemed to me that black fake eye lashes were placed on her closed eyes. Kinda' odd. Weird. I looked long and hard but still couldn't figure it out.

Judy Garland was wearing her wedding gown (so said the New York Post). Her dress was beige or a light taupe. It had a beautiful belt like sash—braided with the taupe dress fabric and intertwined with pearls. I could see the tips of her little satin slippers (bet she had teeny-tiny feet). Judy Garland was wearing her wedding band on her right hand—the custom in Europe.

I don't remember what her casket was made of—cherry? mahogany? walnut? bronze? (I guess I'm exposing my "mortician's daughter" fascination with these things). The front of Judy Garland's casket was covered with flower arrangements so those people paying their respects couldn't get too close to her. That was a good thing.

As I was the last one leaving the chapel, I noticed that Judy Garland's family was entering from a side door—her daughter, Lisa Minnelli with her dad, sister and brother. You'd be proud that I didn't gawk or say a word. That was hard! Yeah, real hard. I paid my respects in a nice, quiet way.

Then I hurried and scurried back to our apartment, undressed in the bathroom, hopped back in bed and never fessed up. Well, maybe later. A couple of weeks later. I'm sooooo happy Judy saw Judy— my namesake.

The Baby Model

After I got married the first time, I went to work for an orthopedic surgeon. (*Orthopedic;* the *medical specialty concerned with correction of deformities or disorders of the skeletal system.*) His office was at East 77th street, in New York City, just a nice walk from our apartment. I was the surgeon's secretary-receptionist— a one- man-band so to speak.

The doctor had the famous comedian, Dom DeLuise, as a patient. OH, what a hoot he was. Dom always called me "Miss Judy". He would rush into our office, lean over my desk and cover me with kisses—sometimes Dom would reach for my left hand and kiss my rings. Many times (well, when his back was better) Dom DeLuise would sit on the edge of my desk and fiddle with my pencils— like playing the drums with them. I'd stop everything, except for answering the phones and we'd chat and carry-on together. The doctor never reprimanded me because when Dom went into his office he too perched himself on the edge of the doctor's desk—and played the drums.

When Dom DeLuise left the office—he'd kiss my rings and say, "Miss Judy— thank you—thank you." He blew a kiss and then blew out the door…

Dom DeLuise occasionally brought me little gifts…maybe a box of chocolates or a sweet bouquet of flowers, which he bought at a florist shop right around the corner—cuz' I recognized the wrap. I loved that man with or without the gifts (but you all know how I love to open gifts.) I couldn't wait until his next appointment with the doctor. Dom DeLuise might have had the best magnetic personality of any man I've ever known—and that's sayin' something.

This leads to a cute little story. And after that, I'll tell you about the baby model. I will try and tie it all together for you.

Years later, after my divorce, I'm back in Pennsylvania and I had a date with Gary Levin. Gary asked me if I'd like to go to "The Valley Forge Music Fair"? Back then, it was a theatre- in-the-round and under a tent—honest. Gary said, "There's a funny funny man, Dom DeLuise, a comedian who's the headliner—would you like to see his show?"

Awe, sure. I'd love to go. I didn't tell my date that I knew Dom DeLuise—it'd ruin the magic and it's always nice to play dumb and make your date feel special.

At the Valley Forge Music Fair and we had great seats—right up in the front row. YES!

Now Dom DeLuise is on center stage doing his funny skit—the one where he's a magician and he's wearing a long black flowing cape and a towering jeweled turban (*Turban; a man's headdress consisting of long cloth wound around the head*). He twirls his black cape round and round and around looking for a volunteer from the audience.

And he stopped at ME.

HOLY CRAP.

Next thing I know, I'm up on the stage with Dom DeLuise. Magically, he put me under his cape—he's under there too—both of us, together under his cape, dancing round and round in circles—full of spirit.

Just like we kids used to sing… "ring around the ro – sie… pocket full of po - sies"…

Then lo' and behold he recognizes me, and says…

"Oh my God, it's you, Miss Judy? Miss Judy – is it REALLY you—from my doctor's office…"

"Yes. Yes. It's me. Miss Judy".

Now we're still dancing around in circles…still under his big black billowing cape. We're holding each other and twirling round and around together—reminiscing—and laughing with joy.

"Darn, Miss Judy, I have to get back to my show now and I can't make you disappear."

Soooo, out I emerged from underneath Dom DeLuise's big black flowing cape. He held my hand and said to the audience—"Let's give Miss Judy a big hand here." Then he kissed my rings, and covered my face with more kisses—just like from long ago in New York City in the doctor's office.

Let's get back to the orthopedic surgeon now…

He was the doctor for the New York Jets Football team. Joe Namath, the hunkie quarterback for the New York Jets, was his patient. Darn it all, I never had a chance to meet Joe Namath. Aww, shucks. I wanted to meet Joe in the worst way—ah, maybe someday.

The doctor was also a joy to work with, and I stayed with him for over a year until about my 8th month of pregnancy. Oh how I hated to leave the doctor and Dom DeLuise.

But about a month later, a wonderful thing happened. I gave birth to Jennifer Louise-Kent Traynor. She was darling with her cute little bow lips and little hair, if any.

Now I must admit, the adjustment of having a newborn and living in New York City, in a rent-controlled apartment building, was a challenge.

We had NO sink in our bathroom—our one small kitchen sink was kept immaculate because we bathed Jennifer in it…brushed our teeth in it…washed all our dishes in it (we had no dishwasher) and I did some laundry in it. Now you try living with a new baby in a tiny apartment with only one sink in the whole place. It stinks.

Also, living in a teeny-tiny apartment, where does one put the stroller? Luckily our apartment was on the first floor and we could chain the stroller to a pipe in the hall. (If we didn't chain it, the next day—POOF—the stroller would be gone.)

The rent-controlled apartment building had no washers or dryers in the building… NADA… none. I would tuck Jennifer in her stroller and schlep heavy tote bags, filled with our dirty laundry, and we'd walk 3 blocks to the nearest laundromat, Mr. Suds. My first time there, I put all of Jen's pretty little clothes (from her baby shower) in the washer. I placed my coins in the silver slots, and we left Mr. Suds. When we returned about 30 minutes later, all her clothes were gone—absolutely gone—somebody had taken her pretty new clothes from the washer, soap suds and all. I was crushed, and couldn't believe someone would do that. So thereafter, we'd sit in that miserable place, Mr. Suds, waiting patiently for our clothes to be washed and then put into the dryer. I hated going there, but I did love being with Jennifer. I held Jennifer, covered her with kisses, played with her on top of the washing machine, sang songs and peek-a-boo— we had a good time together. You do what you have to do. So long, Mr. Suds. See you next week.

All my friends were still working, and I didn't know anybody who was home with a baby. No one. Jen's dad was in law school, so he had to study every night and I couldn't have my friends over, nor would I ask him to watch Jennifer. That's just the way it was. I missed contact with people—as I'm a people person (really!).

What to do? Oh, I know, we'll go to Central Park to the playground—that's where I'll meet new friends. The next day I dressed baby Jennifer in her best pink dress and matching pink bonnet, I tucked a new blanket (the one mother had lovingly made) around her and put Jennifer's Steiff monkey, a new baby gift, in there with her. They looked so cute together—both sharing her pillow.

So off we went to Central Park to the playground to meet new friends.

Oh, happy day.

When we got to Central Park, all I saw were nannies pushing fancy prams, with babies tucked in with their monogrammed ilet blankets—many even had the child's name embroidered on the edge of their scalloped pillow shams, probably Porthault's cotton percale pillow shams.

Whatever. Nobody would talk to me, Lord, I tried. So we slunk home— Jennifer, her monkey and I—without meeting anybody.

It was about that time that I was "blue" or now they call it post-partum depression. I'm sure I had that. I was so happy to have baby Jennifer, but I guess sad for me, because I had nowhere to go except Mr. Suds.

One day I took Jennifer to her pediatrician, or baby doctor. (I was told the doctor was Joan River's pediatrician for her daughter Melissa.) He probably sensed I wasn't quite myself and he said to me, "You know, Judilee, you've got one ugly kid there—an egghead too ('cause she was almost bald). I have a good friend, Marge McDermott, who owns a modeling agency for children. I'll give her a call and I'll get back to you."

Oh, there was hope.

The very next day, Jennifer's pediatrician called me personally to tell me what to do. "Go to McDermott Modeling Agency next Tuesday—that's the day they view the babies." Jennifer and I were there that next Tuesday. Her monkey went along too.

A young mother was in the waiting room with her beautiful boy... black ringlets, big blue eyes and he was dressed in such a handsome expensive looking outfit. She looked over at me and had the nerve to say to me..."You're not taking HER in there to be viewed are you?"

Then the door opened and an assistant chose 5 babies at a time to go into a warm viewing room. "Strip your child—remove all clothes—only keep a diaper on."

We did as we were told and I stood next to that bitch with pretty boy. Marge McDermott, or maybe it was her assistant, came into the warm room, held each child and gave a quick inspection on each baby—and said... "Thank you for coming; you can go, you can go, you can go, you can go and then she stood right in front of Jennifer putting her hand on her head, and said, and you stay, please."

The bitch and pretty boy had to go, and she's standing there arguing with the assistant...and I turned my head, looked at her with such joy and said, "SORRY, Better luck next time."

I was over the moon—I found a payphone and we called mother and daddy with our exciting news. Next I called the pediatrician—and I remember we were cut off because I had no more dimes to feed the pay phone. Darn it all.

McDermott modeling agency quickly told me what to do:

1. Get Jennifer a social security number.

2. Go to the Employment Certificating office—350 Ave. of the American (6th Ave) and get a Child Model Permit.

3. Come back as soon as you've done that.

Eventually, I found out why they hired Jennifer and not pretty boy, and it was because Jennifer was a unisex looking baby (*Unisex; designed or suitable for both sexes.*)—she could represent a boy or a girl. When selling a product, if you had a cute little girl, say with long pigtails (darling Dorie comes to mind), and there was a picture of a boy on the box cover, most likely you wouldn't buy the product. Get it, you had a little girl but the toy or box cover had a picture of a boy.

Sooo long pretty boy—HA-LOW egghead! Go Jennifer.

…Long story short…we signed with McDermott Modeling Agency… and here were their rules:

1. The Agency will call you and you will go to the designated location. The interview is called a 'go-see' that's modeling lingo.

2. If your phone line is busy after many tries and we cannot reach you after 2 days—you will be removed from the agency.

3. If you refuse 3 'go sees' you will be removed from the agency.

Oh Boy, this is life in the fast lane now.

I would just get Jennifer to sleep in her crib—winding her animal mobile—and then the pink wall phone in our kitchen would ring. And it went something like this…

Ring ring ring…

"Hello".

"This is McDermott modeling agency and Jennifer has a 'go see' at Rudy Muller Studios—3185 39th street at 3PM—can you be there ASAP (as soon as possible). There is a product, "Evenflo' Disposable Nurser set, and they're looking for the right baby for a cover."

"Yes. We'll be there."

Now here's the thing—I'd get Jennifer awake from a sound sleep—stuffed my hot pink diaper bag to the gills—grabbed the bus and subway schedule—and away we went. No, we didn't grab a cab—we couldn't afford a cab—so we'd ride the subway, take a bus and do a lot of walking. The whole time I'm holding Jennifer and our bag is stuffed to the brim. My arms were so toned from carrying Jennifer all over New York City—I was in great shape, if I do say so myself.

The studios were usually walk-ups (stairs) and not in the best neighborhoods. Many times I had trouble finding the right building and studio. Hey, Jennifer and the diaper bag were getting to be a load here. And her monkey always came along with us—the monkey's head sticking out of the hot pink diaper bag. It made Jen happy—me too.

Eventually we found the studio—we'd walk up a few flights and then we'd plop ourselves down in a chair along with the other 'hopefuls' and we'd wait our turn to be interviewed. The interviews were short—say 5 minutes—they knew exactly what they were looking for.

"Thank you for coming—we'll be in touch."

So back home we went—Jennifer, monkey, and I—and 10 pounds in my diaper bag. (well, it felt like it.)

And the next day—

Ring ring ring…

"Hello."

"This is McDermott modeling agency, Jennifer has a 'go see' at Warsaw Studio, 40 East 34th Street—2PM they're looking for print ad for Penny's catalog."

"We'll be there."

A few days later…

Ring ring ring…

"Hello"

"This is McDermott modeling agency, Jennifer has a 'go see' at Mat Metsick studio, 450 Park Avenue at 3:15. (Oh, finally, a nice address, on Park Avenue, that'll be easy to find.) There is a company called Creative Playthings and they're looking for print copy for their box covers"

"Thank you. We'll be there."

…And that's how it worked in the big time world (wode) of baby modeling. It was a lot of hard work, but I made lots of nice new friends. I think Jennifer usually got 1 job from 5 "Go sees".

Jennifer's rear end was on the Pampers' box, Evenflo Disposable Nurser set, Penny's and Sear's catalogs (playpens, cribs and musical swings.) Johnson and Johnson Baby Oil (ole) ads, and on most of the box covers for Creative Playthings (Rainbow Twirler, Inquarium, Crawligator)…and so on and so on…

One of my favorite memories, in my whole life, happened just a few years later. We left New York City and moved to Berwyn, Pa. It was around Christmastime, snowing lightly, Jennifer was about 3 or 4 now, all decked out in a red plaid wool coat and matching hat which was trimmed in green velvet. We went to church in Wayne and afterwards we walked the snow covered streets to peek in all the store windows with their colorful Christmas decorations.

At that time there was a fabulous toy store called, Wayne Toy Town, and when we stopped to peek in at their window display—LO AND BEHOLD—boxes and boxes of products by Creative Playthings were in the window—with Jennifer's baby pictures still featured on every single box cover.

Jennifer looked in the window and then looked up at me and said, "Oh, mommy what a cute little baby." And I looked down at her and said… "That's you honey, that's YOUR picture on all those box covers." But she didn't get it—but I got it—and oh how I loved that moment in time.

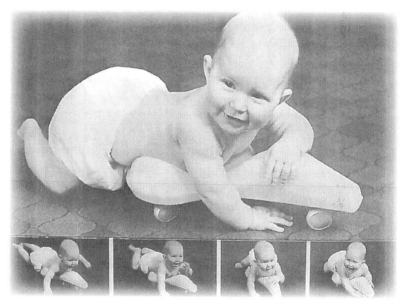

That's Jennifer on the "Crawligator". She got going so fast that she kept going off the hard floor onto the carpet which stopped her. The photographers had to do many, many shoots just to capture this picture. She was having so much fun on her new wheels.

TV Stardom

When I was still working at the Payne Whitney Psychiatric Clinic in New York City, my friends had all been on a popular TV show called "The Match Game". My friend, Leslie, asked me if I'd like to audition for the show.

Are you kidding. Absolutely. That's a big fat YES fer' sure…

So the following week, I went downtown to the location I was given to "try out" for The Match Game Show. The waiting room was jam-packed with all of the hopeful contestants and me. I was hopeful too. First, we all had to fill out a form: name, address, age, phone, profession…. Then someone came and took a Polaroid picture of each wishful contestant. Say cheese. I gave my best smile. Then a nice lady came out and excused about half the hopefuls…hey, I was still in the game.

Next we few remaining contestants-to-be were given 25 questions to answer, i.e., "Who wrote Madame Butterfly?" Answer: Puccini. Hallelujah I knew the first question. A miracle. They probably wanted to know if the would-be contestants had a brain and could put a complete sentence together.

Then, the nice lady returned, collected our papers, and thanked us for coming to be interviewed for The Match Game Show. "We'll be in touch—thank you for coming—we'll be in touch…"

Soooo a few weeks later, an assistant of "The Match Game Show" was in touch and he asked me to come back to the studio for a mock-up, or trial run, of the show.

I went downtown to the TV studio and I DID get chosen for The Match Game Show. YES. YES! Now who'd ah thunk? Not me. No, not really.

Mr. Todman and Mr. Goodson were the producers of that show. They were fabulous producers and great in their craft. They had one hit show after another after another.

Hey, there's a lot of hard work and effort to become a contestant on a TV show. Now I have such appreciation for the contestants on various shows—like Jeopardy—or—The Millionaire with Meredith Vieira. Isn't Meredith down to earth and wonderful. Oh, to have lunch with Meredith one day—I'd love that. My friend, Phyllis Boland, was on Jeopardy. Another friend, Judy White, was on The Price Is Right; she won a mink stole and pots and pans.

…Back to The Match Game TV Show. I was on a panel with Vivian Vance (Ethel from the I Love Lucy Show). Now unless you live under a rock, you've all seen the I Love Lucy Show. You'll laugh out loud watching that show. The other famous celebrity was John Forsythe, the handsome actor from the #1 hit show called, Dynasty. And then there was me. Oh my, oh my. On the other panel—our competition—sat Miss America, Ed McMahon (Johnny Carson's side-kick) and the third contestant was like me, an unknown, but happy to be on the panel. I won't go into how we played The Match Game—but let's just say when they asked me to name a "hard-skinned fruit"—I said "peach." DUH. STUPID. And to this day whenever I hold a nice ripe peach, I smile and think of that Match Game memory. (Oh the answer was orange.)

Well, after The Match Game "wrapped" the producer, said the show would "air" in about 2 months.

Vivian Vance (Ethel) said, "Hey, anyone need a ride? I'm going uptown."

"Hey, I do. I do. I'm going uptown, Ethel, er, Miss Vance. I'm going uptown too". John Forsythe was going uptown, also. Oh, my dreamboat.

There I sat—in the back seat of Ethel's long Lincoln car, floating along, while she drove and chatted with John Forsythe. Ethel had such beautiful skin and hands. She was sooo very lovely and laughed easily. Sitting in the front seat beside her was John Forsythe—now he was one handsome hunk—and just as nice too. There I am still sitting all puffed-up in the back seat of Ethel's Lincoln, thinking ah, darn, we'll soon be there at my street. I wanted to ride in that back seat forever—I was eavesdropping on their conversation. My ears perked up when I heard them talking about famous stars and their lives in showbiz. They forgot about me sitting there in the luxurious back seat.

"Excuse me, excuse me, Ethel, er, Miss Vance, my street is coming up soon. It's 83rd and 3rd Avenue."

"Oh, my dear, I forgot about you darling girl sitting back there. Thank you for being on the panel with John and I. Didn't we have a good time? Did you say 83rd and Third?"

"Yes. My street's 83rd and coming up soon." (Darn it) Now I did not ask for their autographs, that would have been tacky and inappropriate, but I sure wanted their signatures. Besides, who'd ever believe this story?

Ethel pulled over to the curb, and blew me a kiss. John Forsythe looked at me, smiled and waved. Then I got out of her Lincoln and just stood there at that curb waving and waving as they pulled away… they went merrily on their way.

Now let's fast-forward 2 months later…I was visiting my parents in Watsontown. While there I had a sudden kidney infection and was admitted to Geisinger Hospital. I had a roommate and she wasn't too pleasant—she wasn't that sick either—she was not nice. At all. And besides she had the hospital bed by the window, the one with the view. Whatever. I was so sick I really didn't care. (Oh, I take that back, I did care…maybe just a wee bit—I wanted that window view. I wasn't that sick!)

Back then you paid $1.00 or $2.00 a day to have a TV installed in your hospital room. Daddy paid. Now guess what show was coming on at 4pm? THE MATCH GAME. My roommate said, "Now that's a stupid game show. I don't wanna watch it." By then I was so annoyed at her that I told her, "Well, I do and besides my daddy paid for the TV service. So there."

The Match Game came on and there I was larger than life! Moi on the TV sitting next to Vivian Vance (from the I Love Lucy Show) and John Forsythe (from Dynasty). My roommate looked at the TV and turned her head and looked at me lying in my hospital bed. She looked at me again—then back at the TV and said in utter disbelief…OMG. YOU. IS THAT YOU THERE ON THE MATCH GAME SHOW?

"Ah, yeah that's me. Eat your heart out."

After the show was over, my not so nice roomate scooted out of her bed, grabbed a pen and paper and came to my bedside and demanded my autograph. (Imagine that!)

"No way, bitch (I actually said that), I'm not signing my name for you, never ever. So why don't you just hop right back in your hospital bed and read a magazine." And I did not sign my autograph for her, but my heart wore a happy face all night long. ☺

My little story doesn't end here—about a week after we taped "The Match Game Show" I got a call from either Mr. Goodson or Mr. Todman's office (I just don't remember which producer it was). They asked me if I'd be interested, along with my husband, in becoming "professional contestants". I didn't know there was such a thing. In becoming a professional contestant, we would "test out" or "pilot" new upcoming shows for TV. And again, I replied…are you kidding. Absolutely! So Mr. Todman, or was it Mr. Goodson, sent a car for us, gave us money for a nice dinner (beats my tuna casserole) and the producer also paid us for a couple hours as professional contestants. There we were in the TV studio having such a good time playing games that hopefully would one day be on television. We did that for many months.

So there you have it—that's a "wrap" on my TV "Stardom".

Clematis

When I was married to my first husband, we lived in New York City. He worked for McDonald and Co., a brokerage firm in the city. The gracious McDonald's would open up their home – I believe in the Hamptons – for their annual company picnic.

Their beautiful home had many flagstone steps and about every 5th step or so there was a lamp post covered in pink clematis. Now for those of you who are not gardeners, clematis is a vine of the buttercup family having showy flowers.

Well, I finally worked my way up all those steps to the front door passing many lampposts completely covered in beautiful colorful Clematis flowers. Mrs. McDonald was standing there in the doorway, in her long Lilly dress. She extended her hand to me and, as I shook her hand, I said, "Oh, Mrs. McDonald you have the most beautiful clitoris I've ever seen"…

P.S. Mother dear, now well into her 90's, had a purple clematis climbing on her white trellis which she enjoyed from her kitchen window. Every year she'd call us and say "I just wanted you and George to know that my clitoris is in full bloom today!".

Coke in the Cold Room

Harry Staib III was an old friend.

OK, maybe a boyfriend. I dated Harry in high school and then again after my divorce.

Harry loved to come for visits upstairs in the funeral home. We'd sit around our oval table and chat with mother and daddy. We'd laugh, tell some jokes and just enjoy one another.

Sometimes we'd have old-fashioned Coke floats. Ever have one? 1 scoop of vanilla ice cream,   couple of ice cubes and Coca Cola. Stir and fluff it up. Yup, it's refreshing, foamy and mmmm good.

Maybe later the men would switch to something stronger…like whiskey.

Now where was I?...darn it, I always get off the track…My mind gets scattered. Hmmm, scatterbrain comes to mind.

Oh Harry –

Harry was cool. Tall dark and handsome, too. He was self-assured, never hassled and a no worries kind of guy.

Harry could not get over the fact that his old girlfriend, Jackie Crouse, also lived above a funeral home. Mother was a nurse and worked at Divine Providence Hospital. Jackie was a nurse's aide there. Jackie was gorgeous –she looked like Snow White with her black hair and white skin. Mother introduced me to Jackie and that's where I met Harry…

Aye yie yie…

One night—when Harry was visiting—it rained and it poured, dark, teeming rain.

Upstairs, we ran out of Coca-Cola and daddy said, "Hey, Harry, would you mind going downstairs into the cold room, 1st door on your left, and bring up some more Coke? It stays nice and cold down there and it gives Louise more room up here in the refrigerator."

"Hey, no problem, Paul."

So Harry went downstairs, opened the wrong door and walked smack into the preparation room. Harry found himself standing just inches away from a lady on the morgue table. Harry said, her head was resting in a silver-like head rest, her long hair hanging straight down. Right after entering the preparation room, CRACK, went a lightning bolt; light trickled through a row of glass blocks and lit up the entire preparation room.

Upstairs, we thought we heard some noises and carrying-on coming from downstairs…and when Harry returned, white as a sheet, he said, "Hell Paul, forget the damn Coke Float thing—I'll have that whiskey now!"

Together Forever

It was a sad day when my daddy died. It was the day after Frank Sinatra died, so I'd like to imagine that daddy flew to heaven holding onto Frank's tuxedo tails.

I was my daddy's girl— a spoiled brat. He knew it, I knew it and now you'll all know it too. But I'm a nice spoiled brat.

Lee, his dog, would always sleep on daddy's lap – or as mother would say, Lee's your daddy's Peter warmer! Lee was a she—but in no way named after me. Puleeze.

Daddy loved to tell the story of when Lee was a puppy and one day his granddaughter, Jennifer, found Lee's baby tooth next to her slimy dog chew.

"Hey Papa, pronounced paw-paw (that's what Jennifer called him), let's put Lee's little tooth under my pillow and see if the tooth fairy comes tonight".

Soooo – in the morning the tooth fairy came and left a dime and a dog biscuit.

As time marched on the dog got old too. I hate to admit it but Lee was this little old, plump, bow-legged black toy poodle. Ouch. Sorry Lee.

Daddy was a macho man and not a toy poodle kinda' guy. He always had big hunting dogs—but I pawned my dogs off on him. Oh yes, I almost forgot, when I lived in New York City, I had a poodle named Zebonne', pronounced Z-bone, if you please. (A made up name—stupid I know. I was trying my French.) I gave that dog to Aunt Lucille. Ooooh another memory has just surfaced... I had a toy poodle called Gigi—an original name there—I gave her to mother and daddy. Dang, I don't remember how they got Lee—but not from me!

Lee was so old, she had very few teeth left (like summer teeth...you know, some are here, some are there....) the little dog had bad breath and lots of warts. And she'd been sick. Get where we're going here?

It was time.

Since daddy had just died, the family unanimously decided to have Lee cremated and then the dog's ashes were to be placed in a little box to go in the casket with daddy.

Raleigh, my nephew, volunteered (not really) to take the dog to the veterinarian to proceed with our wishes. Two sweet little old ladies were sitting in the waiting room— one holding a fat cat.

"Oh what's your little dog's name?"

"Lee".

"What's she here for?"

Raleigh stammered, stuttered and sputtered and said, "Well, ah, she's, ah here for her shot."

The dog's remains were placed in a miniature tin toy box— actually a cute little box— and she went into the casket with daddy. And the little dog did go to heaven with her master.

Together forever.

Daddy, Lee, and Me

P.S. Before daddy died, he told me he had three wishes.

And here they are…

1. "Take good care of your mother."

2. "I'd like to go to the cemetery in your brother's antique hearse driven by a team of horses."

3. "It'd be nice to be in a solid copper vault. You know, Honeygirl, I never ever sold one, but I sure as hell tried."

P.P.S. And all his wishes came true.

Raspberry and Red

Many times when daddy was downstairs conducting viewings and funerals, I would sit at the top of the staircase looking down watching the mourners (*mourning; the manifestation of sorrow for a person's death. Somber. Gloomy*). People were always coming and going …going and coming from our funeral home. It was a steady stream of darkness. The crying, wailing, and carrying-on from downstairs seeped up the stairs to me. It was so sad. There I sat at the top of the staircase, thinking I was invading their privacy, but still looking downstairs at all the people, coming and going. I never got used to those SAD sad sounds. Never. Ever.

I was always looking down on a sea of dark dreary colors— blacks, greys, navy blue. Of course, the men always wore their dark suits.

Actually, it was so very depressing to see those same dark colors year after year after year. So I said to myself, when I get older I don't want to wear those dark colors which remind me of funerals and death. I'll wear spirited colors— zippy fabrics. Maybe that's probably why I dress the way I dress… colorful. Are you thinking gaudy here? (*gaudy; showy in a tasteless way*).

If you'd open my closet doors and peek inside it looks like a rainbow—a riot of beautiful colors. It makes me happy. Raspberry (hot pink) is my favorite color…a girlie color. I enjoy experimenting with colors—i.e., wearing red and raspberry together. Or cobalt blue and apple green, hmmm, maybe bright yellow with orange. You'll find a lot of leopard in there too, leopard jacket, leopard belts and leopard sweaters. BRRR- love it. Don't you think leopard and red is great together?

Just this past Spring, actually it was Easter time, I wore a new sweater set that I had just purchased at Talbot's in Paoli. They called the color pansy (purplish), like the flower. It is the most beautiful color. I wore the sweater set with some colorful, honkie, big curly Q necklace and carried my lemon yellow bag and got all dolled-up. One of you said, "Oh, Doodie you look just like an Easter egg"... who said that!? Come to think of it, I WAS very colorful and I probably looked like the eggs in their baskets.

You will not find any navy or very little grey, in my closet. I do enjoy black in the wintertime and love to throw on a pair of jeans, paired with a black cashmere turtleneck and a big belt. I'll plop a black beret on my head... then I'm good-to-go and I'll come see you. So keep the door open.

Maybe you all don't know this but in the old days—way back centuries ago—when a loved one died, the ladies wore black for mourning. They wore black for one year and often longer. In fact, after Queen Victoria's husband, Prince Albert, died she wore black for the rest of her life. (Oh, I'd go nuts). Black has always been symbolic of death. In more recent years it has become acceptable to wear colors to funerals. At daddy's funeral, we requested no dark colors, please.

And no dark clothes to my funeral either...

Or I'll sit up and scare you. (But I'll be in raspberry and red!)

P.S. ... And on my Tombstone— She Lived
She Loved
She Laughed
She Left

A Lovely Lady

Everybody used the exact same adjective to describe my mother. And the word is LOVELY. I have often heard, "your mother is a lovely lady." And she is. My friends often said, "Judilee, when I grow up I want to be just like your mother." Her name is Louise Ariminta Cronrath. Although, mother's not too crazy about her middle name Ariminta, not even a little. (She was named after a rich old auntie who didn't leave her a single cent!)

You grandchildren and now great grandchildren call her MAMA, pronounced maw-maw (or as Connor, then age 7, spells it MALL MALL!). Well, mother did like to shop at the mall.

When mother was a little girl, she and her siblings grew up on a farm just outside Danville, Pa. They all attended a one-room schoolhouse that was maybe a mile or two from the farm. It was grades 1 thru 7. The teacher would sit at her desk right up in front of the room. And behind her desk there was a large chalk board, the length of the room. Above the chalk board, there was the alphabet in beautiful cursive script - or the ABC's.

The teacher would sit at her desk, at the front of the room, and she'd call classes 1st thru 3rd to come sit up in front with her while grades 4th thru 7th sat at the back of the school room doing their homework or taking tests. Then the grades would rotate again. And again…go to the front of the room with the teacher - and then - go to the back of the one-room schoolhouse to study.

Mother remembered she liked to sit in the back of the one-room schoolhouse, because the pot-bellied stove was there and it was a lot warmer in the back. The boys would take turns putting wood into the pot-bellied stove (that is, when the boys weren't spinning the globe while the teacher was out of the room). Mother remembered, "they liked that job…they kept warm."

Occasionally, at recess, mother had the honor of ringing the schoolhouse bell which told the children to come back inside the school house. "I remember when I pulled the large rope to ring the bell. The rope was thick and it had a big knot at the end. Sometimes it was hard to ring that bell, but I always did it. I was proud to ring the school bell."

In the winter time, sometimes her mother would take her to school in a cutter sleigh *(Cutter; a small light sleigh, usually drawn by one horse)*. Mother and her brother and sisters also walked to school on the hard crust that formed on top of the snow. Mother said, "It was really like walking on a road as our feet never fell through the snow. Those were different times back then." I remember asking mother what they did for fun, like on a Saturday, "you know mother, back in the good ol' days?"

Mother said, "The kids from town would love to come out to the farm. Well, we'd skate on the pond, then when we got tired of skating, we'd coast (sled) down the hill. When we got so cold that our mittens got stiff—then we'd come inside. Maybe we'd have hot chocolate with marshmallows and cookies. Always cookies from grandma's tin. We might even play games like Pit, Parcheesi, or Jacks; it just depended on how many kids came to the farm. But we always gathered around the piano and I played all their favorite songs and we'd all sing together. Many times, the same songs over and over again. And again. Ah, such fun we all had on the farm—they never wanted to leave, they really didn't."

…And now you grandkids ask me… "Hey, Doodie, what was it like in the good old days?" When I tell you we had no TV, dishwasher, microwave, cell phones, and laptops - your eyes glaze over!

Now back to mother…

Mother was proud to be a graduate of the Reading Hospital, Class of 1934. It was during the Depression and times were tough. When she went off to nurses' training, mother was given a pair of beat-up second-hand shoes that were a size too small. "They really didn't fit me very well." (Hey, maybe that's why I'm a little sensitive about my feet). Mother wore black stockings and those old second-hand shoes all throughout nurses' training. At graduation, when she received her hard-earned RN (Registered Nurse) degree, mother could then and only then, wear white stockings, a sign that she was now a nurse. "My white stockings had seams, too. Oh, how happy I was." And as a graduation gift she received a new pair of white shoes to go with her white stockings and new white uniform. Back then, nurses only wore white - absolutely no colors were allowed. Oh how times have changed!

The graduate nurses from Reading Hospital all received navy wool capes, a hospital pin, which would be worn on her white uniform over her heart, and mother's prized possession, her starched white nurse's cap. Mother's cap was a traditional one, the kind you see in the movies. One could identify the nursing school where one graduated, by the cap a nurse wore. Some caps looked like a cup cake sitting on top of their heads, other caps were ruffled and some even looked like 'the flying nun' with large wings. Oh I do have many memories of mother actually boiling her nurses cap in sugar water (in a pan on top of the stove) to make her cap stiff. She'd remind me to "keep an eye on my cap, Judilee, so it doesn't boil (bole) down."

Years later, mother proudly wrapped her cap, her most prized possession, and gave it to Jodi when she graduated from Thomas Jefferson School of Nursing. Now Jodi cherishes mother's nurse's cap and one day maybe she'll pass it on to another nurse in the family.

Throughout her life, mother helped so many people with her compassion and wonderful nursing skills. Mother especially loved pediatrics: *(Pediatrics; a branch of medicine concerned with the care of children).*

That's where she met her all-time favorite patient, Jimmie Frasso.

Jimmie was around 14 or 15 years of age when he was admitted to the Reading Hospital with pneumonia. Mother said, "He was a very sick boy." Jimmie adored mother (well, who didn't). He called her Nurse Happy. From that day forward for the next 60+ years, every single year in the summertime, Jimmie Frasso would visit mother for a day. "He'd come early and he stayed late." Jimmie would bring his girlfriends to meet mother and he would not get married until Nurse Happy approved of his choice.

Then Jimmie came with his children and various dogs. I do remember a dog named Gigzy. She peed everywhere! And I don't think Gigzy was invited back the following year. So there you have it... Jimmie Frasso, never missed a sunny summer day with his Nurse Happy.

Mother (Mama) came to Watsontown, Pa. as a private duty nurse. And that's where she met daddy (Papa).

They married in 1937 and they bought a double house on Main Street that they eventually turned into the Cronrath Funeral Home which remains today. Then mother had my brother Gary and a few years later I came bouncin' in. And I'm still bouncing all around!!...

Back in those days—1940's and 1950's—mother kept to a strict routine as all the mothers of that generation did. Mother would...

- Wash on Monday
- Iron on Tuesday
- Bake on Wednesday
- Clean on Thursday
- Market on Fridays
- Sew on Saturday
- Go to church on Sunday

Ah yes, Monday, mother's wash day. Now here's a cute story…

Living above the funeral home, on the second floor, mother would hang her wash on a pulley clothes line: *(Pulley; a moving cable or rope that rides in a groove in its edge)*. That pulley clothes line stretched across the backyard and attached to the garage. Try to follow here. There was a little narrow porch on the second floor at the back of the funeral home that had a pulley which stretched waaaay across the backyard and attached to the second floor of the garage. Yes, daddy built a large brick garage with a second floor where he had his casket showroom. The pulley or mother's clothes line, obviously had 2 lines—one goin' and one coming back. The area where mother stood to hang her laundry had just enough room for her to stand and stoop down to gather her wet wash from a large wicker basket.

Have I lost you yet?

Mother kept her clothes pins in two large pockets of her zippy red and white polka dot apron. The pockets of mother's apron were edged in white rick rack: *(Rick rack, a narrow zigzag braid used as trim)*. Isn't that a funny word, rick rack. I always loved mother's cute red and white polka dot apron and one day, she gave it to me. I was very happy and proud to wear her apron. On that particular day mother set about hanging out her work of art, i.e., her laundry. Mother always hung the heavy clothes first: like towels, trousers, and jeans. Then next she'd fill the pulley clothes line with sheets, pillow cases, bras and panties. She completely filled the pulley from our second floor to the garage.

Then suddenly it started to get windy. Real quick. Whooosh. And blustery. We could even see the tree tops swaying underneath mother's clothes line. UH OH. The laundry started whipping, snapping and blowing all around. The sheets and bras on the two lines were caught up in each other. WHOOOSH…(So how does one describe blowing?) Daddy came to the rescue, standing on the second floor porch trying his darndest to untangle the laundry which was still wildly blowing and flapping every which way. Finally, daddy had to call the Watsontown Fire Company and they sent the Hook and Ladder truck. The firemen came and untangled the mess on mother's clothes line. They were high to the sky on this rescue. Luckily there were no sirens: *(siren; an acoustical device that produces a loud piercing sound).*

Thereafter, every time a fireman from the Watsontown Fire Company saw mother, they'd say, "Hey, Louise, you washin' today? I'll hang around the hose house (fire house) just in case you need us." Or, "Weezie, are you still washing on Mondays? I'll be sure to stick around and wait for Paul's call."

Speaking of cleaning on Thursdays…we lived in a 3 story funeral home and it's a lot to take care of and mother didn't have much help. I was little help. Well, that's not entirely true; mother had Marguerite Kuhn, who came to help her clean. Marguerite was a poor old soul - a never married, no family kinda' lady. She came every Thursday. And every Thursday I'd greet Marguerite and say, "Hello, Marguerite how are you today?" And she'd reply, "Ohhhh - not so bad." After she was finished cleaning, I'd drive Marguerite home. "How was your day, Marguerite?" "Ohhhh, not so bad." She lived in a teeny tiny house back in the alley, like a little doll house. And I always wanted to get inside. But I didn't. Darn it all.

When Marguerite Kuhn came to clean on Thursdays, I'd get a little annoyed. Now here's why.

Poor Marguerite was so clumsy (like me!) and she was always breaking things. Soooo, mother decided she should only dust and sometimes maybe vacuum. Occasionally, Marguerite Kuhn would start downstairs in our funeral home dusting and vacuuming. But she would only go down stairs if no "guests" were down there in the casket. She was so damn slow, why it'd take her forever just to vacuum one room down stairs in our funeral home. Besides Marguerite usually ran over the vacuum cord and daddy would get the black tape out and repair the cord. There was always something. So guess who did all the hard work? Mother did. Mother was the one on her hands and knees, cleaning the floors, bending over scrubbing the tub and making the sinks and windows sparkle.

Now you see, I thought it should be the other way around. It was like a role reversal. After all Marguerite Kuhn WAS the cleaning lady. You know, one day Marguerite Kuhn was downstairs in the funeral home, but this time she was the one in the casket. We picked a pretty bouquet of roses from daddy's rose garden and we gave Marguerite a good send off. Yes we did.

(Marguerite wasn't feelin' too bad this time). Now here is an opportunity for a wonderful poem by S.R. Hole. It's about roses.

"He who would have beautiful roses in his garden must have beautiful roses in his heart. He must love them well and always. He must have not only the glowing admiration, the enthusiasm, and the passion, but the tenderness, the thoughtfulness, the reverence, the watchfulness of love."
~S.R. Hole~

Now, on a happier note…

Mother is not only a "lovely lady" she is a wonderful mother. She was always there for me through all my adventures...and, oh my, there were so many adventures...boyfriends, weddings, miscarriage, the birth of Jennifer and Gregory, moves, divorce and remarriage. I was the talker and she was a great listener—a magical combination for both of us. It worked.

Now this will surprise you about mother. Mama.

She reads the scandal papers (tabloids) like the GLOBE and NATIONAL ENQUIRER. Who'd ah thunk! Now didn't you ever wonder who reads those trashy papers? My lovely mother does. She wouldn't even buy the scandal papers in Watsontown for fear someone might see her. And God forbid someone would bump into her... So mother would drive to the next town and purchase her "reading material", as she called it. Mother would tell the shop keeper her daughter was coming to town and her daughter enjoyed reading the STAR, NATIONAL ENQUIRER...

That's a crock! In other words, mother sorta' blamed the shame on me.

Then when George and I would come to town for a visit, mother would get me aside and whisper quietly, "I have your 'reading materials' in your room, under your bed."

Yeah, hidden under the bed. I bet when we move the bed, we'll find layers of mother's "reading material" under there— cripes, it could be holding up the springs!

Mother always had crossword puzzles for Georgie Porgie.

Hey, there's something wrong with this picture here. Ah, George with his crossword puzzles and me with the National Enquirer. Hmmm...

Whatever.

I think mother likes George better than me.

Her face lights up whenever she sees George.

The men always went bonkers over mother.

What's not to like. She never talks about herself but is always interested in you. She's a good listener, always wears a smile and is an absolute joy to be around. It's the magic combination. We should all try it.

Mother and George like the same foods too. Especially lemon sponge pie - not lemon meringue – but good ole Pennsylvania Dutch lemon sponge pie. Now George never ever baked a pie (nor me for that matter) but he went online, found a recipe and baked a lemon sponge pie for his mother-in-law. (Now don't you feel the love here?) And that is the only time that I can ever remember mother would not share a piece of her pie. Not a piece. At all. She hid it in the refrigerator. George baked a pie for mother on most visits. See, he was her favorite.

Eventually daddy retired and sold his funeral home to my brother. Then mother and daddy moved to a darling brick home, a rancher, on the outskirts of Watsontown. It is such a bright sunny home with a beautiful view.

George and I loved visiting them. The four of us would go out to dinner, mother and George went antiquing looking for bargains or the girls would shop at the mall or in Lewisburg while the boys watched games on TV. Whatever we did together, we enjoyed each other. Well, except for our bridge games. (Bridge is a card game, an old fogies' game, not the one that goes over the water.) Daddy would say to George, "Hey let's set up the card table and whip the girls again in a game of bridge. What do you say George. We beat them the last time didn't we?!"

Oh, NO WAY Jose.

So the men would have a whiskey and I'd have a glass of wine and shuffle the deck, deal the cards and let the good times roll. They always thought they won that game of bridge and mother and I let the boys think they won. Not really. But we sure had a good time together.

Now here's something thoughtful that mother would always do and maybe you will too. I hope so. When we'd be in a restaurant or anywhere for that matter and we had to use the restroom, many times a cleaning lady might be there working away. Mother would look at her and comment on what a nice job she was doing and how everything sparkled. In my life's observations, most people find the cleaning people invisible. And this applies to the waitresses too. It's a tough job being on your feet all day, serving people and making "nice". I was once a waitress so I do appreciate their efforts and am a big tipper. So be kind and say "hello" - acknowledge their presence please— then flash a big smile.

Back to the restroom... You know when you wash your hands with that white foamy soap and then wave your hands frantically in front of the paper towel dispenser hoping a paper towel will drop down... 'course as the water is slowly trickling down your arm? Ever have that happen? After drying her hands, mother would always make sure another paper towel would drop down and be there for the next person. She was always thinking of someone else. Why don't you do that next time you're in the restroom. Your thoughtful gesture will make the next person happy. It doesn't take much.

As time marches on so do we all. When Mother was 94 and living by herself, she was frightened to stay alone in her house. She suggested "maybe it's time now to go to the home. I don't want to be a burden to my family."

It just so happens we have great friends, Fred and Gini Kessler, who own Nottingham Village, a lovely retirement community with many levels of care. And that's where mother went, to Nottingham Village.

Or as mother said to me with her usual humor, "I'm going to the home and nobody's home here." Even then, mother always looked on the sunny side of life.

So mother left her pretty, cozy brick home with the half-moon driveway, to share a room with a lady she never met before. Mother's name is Louise and her roommate's name is Louise.

Mother looked at me and said, "thank heavens, Judilee, we both have the same name - I think I can remember that."

If you've ever moved a loved one to 'a home' it is gut wrenching. It took all the air out of my balloon and George's too. When I returned home I had a panic attack over it. It was also such an adjustment for mother. In the first week or two, mother barricaded her door with a little chest, and then she'd call 911 "for company". During the next several months mother would call us and say "I just got discharged and I can go back home now. Please come and pick me up."

Not long before mother went to Nottingham Village, I asked mother how she wanted to be remembered. She thought for a while and replied, "I'd like to be remembered as a kind and caring person." And I said, "Oh mother that's so nice, you want to be remembered as a kind person." And mother looked at me, almost pointing her index finger at me and said, "No, that's not what I said, Judilee, I'd like to be remembered as a kind and caring person."

And that's just what mother is, a kind and caring person and A LOVELY LADY, too.

Louise's Life's Little Instruction Book

(This was on mother's invitation for her 80th birthday party.)

- Go to bed happy, wake up happy
- Eat right
- Do something nice for somebody every day
- Have interest in others
- Life is short, eat more pot pie and go shopping
- Be on time
- Keep your hair fluffed
- Play bridge with life-long friends
- Be there to listen
- Positive thinking is strong medicine
- Pray
- And take time to smell the roses.

Sleepin' With the Dog

When I separated, I lived alone with Jennifer and Gregory in a big house, a really big house, on Upland Way in Wayne. The home had maybe six or seven bedrooms and the most beautiful winding staircase you've ever seen, like in the famous movie, 'Gone With the Wind.' Maybe even prettier. The foyer (*foyer; entrance hall*) was so grand and huge that Greg and his friends played hockey in there. When I got divorced and later moved to a little house, I called it my doll house. That little house could have fit in the foyer of the big house. I swear. No exaggerations here. Hard to believe.

In the big house, there was even a fireplace in the foyer—banked on either side with built-in benches. It was quite a charming little nook (*nook; any remote or sheltered spot, as in a room*). Many times I'd sit there in that little nook, and watch Greg play hockey. Or, Jennifer and I would hang out, eat cookies, have Coke floats and read our books together.

I remember sitting on that fireside bench late at night, alone, and crying and wondering what would we do and where would we go; in other words, having a pity party for one.

To try to lift my spirits, I'd sit on that fireside bench, in the foyer (on a green tufted cushion—the green buttons hurt our butts) and imagine

Judilee's Jubilee

myself descending the winding staircase, very very slowly— like that Carol Burnett skit (a famous comedienne). She had a brass drapery rod with green draperies, hangin' over her shoulders…like a ball gown. Carol Burnett, proudly and with perfect posture, descended her "Gone With The Wind" Staircase. Remember that skit? It was funny. You may have seen the reruns of "The Carol Burnett Show". FYI, that "green drapery dress" is now in the Smithsonian Institution in Washington, DC.

Soooo now I pretended to be Carol Burnett descending MY "Gone With The Wind" staircase. I tied a queen size sheet around my neck, and I, too, descended down my beautiful staircase just like Carol Burnett.

Pathetic wasn't it.

The visual still brings a smile. Well, maybe a little smile, but my lips are turned up.

Hey, now where in the heck was I going with this dog story here?

Oh, now I remember, I was scared to death living with two small children in this huge three story old home. The house sat up on a little hill and had many French doors. One of my friends, Ginny said, "So why don't you get a dog? The barking will probably keep the boogie man away."

Hey thanks.

Now you'd think that a girl who lived above a funeral home, her whole life, wouldn't be afraid of anything? Even the boogie man? NOT SO. I was a scaredy cat. But Jennifer and Gregory never knew that their mother was a scaredy cat.

Now what to do?… and what kind of dog to get. I had poodles (which I gave to mother and daddy) and a Yorkie and they wouldn't keep the boogie man away. They were yippie dogs. A yippy yorkie—named

Corkie. We called him Corkie the Yorkie—and he was as dumb as a stone. Once I took Corkie to the vet, Dr. Huggler, for psychological testing. And when I went to get Corkie the Yorkie at the vet, Dr. Huggler said to me, "Judilee, I think you just got yourself a dummy."

So I went to Braxton's, a pet shop in Strafford, and told Mr. Braxton my situation. I'm all alone with two kids in a big house that has many French doors and windows; easy to break into…scared stiff. I think maybe I even started to cry. (You know how your lip quivers and you're trying to hold back the tears—I was there). Mr. Braxton, oh, he was such a wonderful and kind man, leaned down and he hugged me and said, "Don't worry, we'll find you the perfect dog. There are two breeds that might intimidate people and would make you feel safe."

Can you guess what two breeds Mr. Braxton suggested?

Aw come on, think about it. What dog would you be afraid of? Certainly not a Chihuahua. (*ChiWAWA; a very small dog*).

Give up? Humor me here.

Aww, o-kaay—the answer is a German Shepard or a Doberman.

Jennifer and Gregory chose the shepherd and they named her Pepper. Actually they were hinting for another shepherd and they'd call her Salt. Ah, no thanks. Maybe later.

After I kissed and tucked Jen and Greg into bed at night, hours later, I too went to bed. With the dog. Pepper hopped right on top of the bed with me. She always slept on the side not next to the bathroom. She was smart. And Pepper was even under the covers with me, with her head on her own down pillow. (I know what you're thinking—sicko.)

There's more—I'd pet and tuck Pepper in bed, too. I might have hugged her (Ok kissed her is more like it) and wished her pleasant dreams. Do you think dogs dream? I do remember being so very lonely and reaching under the covers to hold Pepper's big paws. Well, we did keep each other warm. Occasionally, during the night, in the wee hours, I'd hear soft snoring and in the dark—looked next to me—and saw a big lump and thought, gosh, ah, a man's in my bed! YIPPEE! And then I saw those big dog ears sticking out from under the blue comforter and then I remembered—I was sleeping with the dog.

That's Jennifer's special birthday card to me. It kinda' says it all.

Lunch Bunch

The Lunch Bunch: left to right; Me, Franny Blair, Ardyth Sobyak, Dolly Somers, Susan Brown, Judy White, Jeanne Honish

When I was going through a divorce and moving from my large house, on Upland Way, to a small "doll house" on Oak Terrace, my girlfriends came to help me pack and get ready to move.

Course you all know, I have two children, Jennifer and Gregory. We packed their rooms and all their treasures with great care. Divorce—it's such an adjustment for everybody—especially for children.

I told the girls I'd have lunch for them, it'd be either turkey or tuna fish sandwiches.

Oooh…yes, they do like my tuna fish, so that's what I'll serve along with home-brewed ice tea and chips. Just come any time after 10.

And they came—six of my girlfriends.

You all might find this hard to believe, because I hate to cook— I have absolutely no self-confidence in the kitchen… But I DO have a signature tuna fish salad recipe.

Who knew. You knew because I always have it.

Why don't I just give you the recipe now before I forget. You'll have to determine the quantities so I'll just give you the ingredients.

Judilee's Tuna Fish Salad

- Can of solid white Albacore Tuna (I like Costco)
- Using a fork-mush it up- then add fresh pepper. A lot.
- Add 1 can of water chestnuts, diced and drained— or perhaps a peeled diced apple instead.
- Add relish
- Add mayonnaise
- Fresh parsley (try to use fresh – or dried is ok too…Ah, not really)
- Celery, optional.

The secret of my Tuna fish is not too much mayo-keep it on the dry side—yet more mayo than relish.

Enjoy! Have me over!

…And now that you have my recipe—let's get back to the story…

We had our luncheon out on the terrace and my tuna fish sandwiches were such a hit.

Actually I cut off the crust and made triangle tea sandwiches and placed them on a pretty white pedestal dish.

TA DAH!

We had such a good time—even during a bad time.

We all said we'd get together again real soon and decided to call ourselves the "Lunch Bunch."

…Now it's 30 some years later and we've lost two of our bunch—Susan Brown and Franny Blair. Ahhh, SAD. I miss you two.

But we still get together in the summertime and so far, I've never missed a year.

The Lunch Bunch meets at Judy White's beautiful home on Long Beach Island, N.J. We enjoy two nights together— we come early and stay late. (I bet Judy's thrilled!)

Our husbands or boyfriends ask us…"What the hell do you girls do all day?"

Wellll, we hoot-en-holler, read current magazines, tell our horoscopes from the Philadelphia Inquirer, shop, bike, paint our toe nails (Ardyth's job) walk and talk, talk and walk, drink, watch movies, fart (excuse me, underleg noises) and last but never the least—we go to the beach looking for shells for our Annual Shell Contest.

Ah, the shell contest— I LOVE that contest...which is very competitive— and I'm competitive.

You betcha'.

I'm not proud of that trait, but it is what it is and I am who I am.

The Shell contest goes something like this:

1. Go to the beach and collect your shells.
2. Arrange your shell entry on a white paper plate.
3. Name your shell entry.
4. Have the 'hunk' from next door come and judge.
5. Announce the winner.

Hey, I won one year! I had a row of white scallop shells with one black scallop shell in the middle of the row—AND— the title was... "Black Sheep of the Family."

Jeanne's shell entry was good— one year she made a mound of wet sand (like a giant ant hill) and placed the little shells coming around the sand mound..., and her title was... "Shell Be Comin' Around the Mountain."

And Jeanne won with her entry. As she should.

Ah, then you have our hostess, Judy, who had 2 large shells—one shell was cracked and the other shell was nice—and— the title was... "Perfect and Not So Perfect" (personally, between you and me, I didn't think hers was that good.)

AH, Boo Hiss—

Judy won that year—but we think she bribed the hunk-judge from next door.

Judilee's Jubilee

C'mon, Judyann, fess up here?

You had the nerve to repeat your "Perfect and Not So Perfect" entry a few years later and— won again! It was rigged. Or I'm a sore loser—that's more like it. Franny had a great idea for her shells. She had a pile of seaweed and she placed two shells on either side of the seaweed, and a small shell was placed in the middle. And her title was… "Little Dick." Get it. I guess you had to be there.

Franny wouldn't enter her creation because she thought she might offend the judge.

Wuss.

Well, before you know it, our 2 days have evaporated and it's time to pack our duffles and head home with another year of memories.

You know everyone should have a group and name it something—even if it's just 2 girls and call yourselves 'the Two-Fers'.

Even George (Skipper) has a group since his high school days—called the Kwami's (Kids Without Any Moral Instruction.) His guy friends are scattered all over the United States and the Kwami's get together every few years. This year we're driving to Idaho to attend a Kwami's reunion. Ah, another adventure. I can't wait.

Back to Lunch Bunch – you kids and grandchildren make some fun. Who knows—maybe one day you'll get a group of wonderful girls together and call your group the Lunch Bunch—or a great bunch of guys and call yourselves the Kwami's.

Go for it!

The Little Orange Dress

When I was living in New York City, I decided I wanted to become an interior designer. It was something I enjoyed and it would be a nice profession when I got older. Like now. So I enrolled at the New York School of Interior Design.

My parents said, "That'll be something to fall back on, Judilee, just in case you ever have to go back to work."

Soooo, many years and 2 children later and a lot of long hours and hard work, I finally received my diploma from The New York School of Interior Design. My diploma even has these purple satin triangle thingys on each corner… in a leather fold-over case too, I might add.

Hallelujah!

Finally, I did it. I think Jennifer and Gregory had a party for their mother, maybe a tea party? We did have homemade cookies with sprinkles on top. I remember they were red, white and blue sprinkles—the kids loved them. We even had Coke Floats with colorful straws. Well, we had a little party, that's for sure!

Shortly after that I did become a single parent.

And back to work—as an interior designer. Mother and daddy were right.

Then I hung out my shingle, PIZZAZZ, and was open for business (or as daddy would say BIDNESS! Mike Boland always loved to say BIDNESS since he knew that was the way many people in our part of Pennsylvania say that word). I was ready to roll – I was now in BIDNESS.

One of my very first clients was Dee and Olav Urheim.

Dee was interviewing interior designers for "a very small project." And I thought, Hmmmm, maybe this could be a start and perhaps lead to a bigger project down the road. You have to start somewhere...right?

I do remember the day of my interview with Dee Urheim. As a single parent—I had a lot goin' on...i.e., found mice droppings in my silverware drawer (under the forks), our dog was limping on three legs, what time is Greg's hockey practice?, when is Jen to be at Elizabeth Jefferson's?, what to have for dinner tonight?, and my rear tire on my white station wagon was slowly going flat. BUT, my wagon's license plate was "PIZZAZZ".

Now that was cool!

Ah, speaking of cool...another license plate I saw said TWOO WUV (get it? True love) But the best license plate I've ever seen was a blonde bombshell driving a fancy sports car that sported her plate HE PAID.

Now back to what to wear for my interview with the Urheims...

I probably opened my closet and grabbed the first bright thing that spoke to me.

An orange dress. You didn't think I'd show up in a sweet little white blouse, wearing a strand of pa-pa-pa-err-ls (darn-it, I still can't say that word), or a simple black pencil skirt, did you?

Actually I'm proud of one thing—I'm always on time—so if I'm even 15 minutes late you know something's up. I do not appreciate people who are always late. I find it rude, thoughtless and inconsiderate and usually I don't tolerate it. Don't have to—they wouldn't be picked as my friend. Amen.

However, I would make one exception, though, for Elizabeth Taylor (the famous movie actress). Liz Taylor was always late—even 15 minutes late for her own funeral, as per her instructions. And wasn't she fabulous. Elizabeth Taylor was a dedicated worker, a philanthropist, doing things for other people (*Philanthropy, concern for human beings manifested by donations to institutions advancing human welfare*). Especially her AIDS crusade for the gay community. Elizabeth Taylor was a pioneer in her AIDS crusade before it became accepted. Speaking of gays— I love them–I worked with so many gay guys in my interior design "bidness". Oh my word, gays are so fun— they're interesting, enthusiastic, creative, impeccably dressed, buff, thoughtful…well, using a French word to sum them up—they have such *joie de vivre;(joie de vivre: a delight in being alive).*

A lot of my gay friends are gone now. One of my doctors, Dr. John, is gay—and he's fabulous. Dr. John's favorite color is 'eggplant' and I love to see what tie he's wearing—besides, he has Chiclet teeth, like the gum (rows of perfect white teeth). I go once a year—and this is one doctor I'm happy to see. And I always wear purple.

So if any of our family is gay—no worries here—I'll be your biggest cheerleader. For sure.

Now where was I? Oh yes, back to my interview with Dee Urheim and I'm about to ring her front door bell…

Ring… Ring…Ring…

Dee opened her door to greet me and there I stood in a bright orange dress, with matching fingernails and toe nails. The orange dress was strapless; the fabric was terrycloth—or let's just say I was wearing a strapless beach cover-up.

My necklace was a huge brass lion's head doorknocker type necklace. Geez, I wonder if I was wearing the matching knocker earrings too! I looked like a cross between a hooker and a floozy.

Hey, I'm even embarrassed to write this. What was I thinking?

Dee wanted the designer-of-choice to select fabrics to reupholster her two large club chairs which were in her living room in a color she <u>did not</u> particularly like. Her chairs were orange velvet.

We matched.

Soooo, I must have done some fast-talking or maybe she felt sorry for me (that's more like it) because I was later hired for the job.

Eventually, I redecorated their entire home and many years later 'refreshed' their home again.

The interior design "bidness" served me well and I eventually participated in five Designer Vassar Show Houses here on the Main Line. Some of my rooms were even featured in national magazines. Our own home was on a House Tour in support of the Devon Horse Show, a fund raiser for the Bryn Mawr Hospital. I was fortunate to decorate homes in New York, New Jersey and Connecticut, as well as Pennsylvania, before retiring. But I'm so happy our children (egads, and now grandchildren) still call upon me for decorating ideas. By the way, when I completed a job, my clients could always find a little life-size metal lady bug (mounted on a straight pin) hidden in their décor, perhaps on a dust ruffle, on the edge of a pillow sham, or the bottom hem of a custom made shower curtain.

Who'd ah thunk! Not in my wildest dreams…

Just last week, Dee and I had lunch together, and she has become a most wonderful friend. I love Dee. And all because of one fast-talkin' hoochie momma wearing a bright orange dress.

Oh, What a Wedding

George and I were married June 8, at 8 in 1984, the hottest day of the year. We were blending a family together. George had 3 children: Don, Dale, and Jodi.

I had two children, Jennifer and Gregory Traynor. We even had a fur family! The groom had a little dog, called Molly. The bride had a big dog, called Pepper. Our five children were our attendants. The boys were handsome in tuxes and the girls were pretty in pink.

I sent out fancy-dancy invitations too.

Our new blended family; Jennifer Traynor, Greg Traynor, the groom, the bride, Don Bennyhoff, Dale Bennyhoff, Jodi Bennyhoff

Judilee's Jubilee

> Judilee C. Traynor
>
> And
>
> George R. Bennyhoff
>
> And
>
> Their children
>
> Invite you to share in the celebration of their marriage on
> Friday, the eighth of June
>
> Nineteen hundred and eighty-four
>
> At eight o' clock in the evening
>
> United Methodist Church
>
> Wayne, Pennsylvania

And the separate small card read:

> Reception
> Nine o' clock to midnight
> Radnor Valley Country Club
> Villanova, Pennsylvania
>
> R.S.V.P
> 316 Oak Terrace
> St. Davids, Pennsylvania 19087

I used R.S.V.P. which means: Respondez s'il vous plait (French, for reply if you please.) But, I did not include a response card which forced everyone to send me their acceptance or regret in writing. I bet the guests hated to respond to me in that way, but there was a reason to my madness. I'm a stationery freak. I wanted to enjoy every person's stationery or note card and have them R.S.V.P. back to me. (And I did and I've saved every one.) Oh, the stamps were 20 cents in 1984 and we used a beautiful floral stamp that spelled LOVE.... ahhh.

Our wedding invitations were white, heavy stock (meaning like cardboard - the thicker the paper the better.) And get this, the color of the ink was in raspberry with the envelopes fully-lined in raspberry. Nuttin' but the best. I'm sure I drove the stationery department nuts trying all different shades of raspberry ink; some shades were too hot-pinkish, other shades were mauve like the interior of the caskets that daddy sold. Yuck!! But we worked hard to get just the perfect shade of raspberry ink, and we did. And the bride was happy. Hmm, maybe I'll use the exact same color for the cover of this book – or maybe not.

My daddy walked me down the aisle. He was wearing a pink tie and mother looked lovely in lilac chiffon. I wore pink, too, with a wide Elvis-like soft leather belt. My belt was handmade in white kid leather and encrusted with pearls and Swarovski crystals. Woo Hoo. $$.

Sorta' like a hunka-hunka burning love belt!

I always liked Elvis.

Suky Rosan, of Bryn Mawr (think high-fashion bridal) made my dress. Suky was a fashion icon. "She was loved for her personal touch and innate ability to find the perfect dress for every woman who shopped there", as was written in The Philadelphia Inquirer.

But what to do for a headpiece? Suky said she'd create something fabulous. Perhaps my headpiece would be hand-wired and covered in Swarovski crystals and pearls. My headpiece would complement my belt. "Maybe a cap-like headpiece going from above your left ear and ending below your right chin," said Suky.

"Ok Suky, sounds good to me. Go for it… do your thing!" Now this was a significant financial and emotional investment. I'll never ever tell you the price of either my headpiece or the Elvis belt. (Only Suky knows!)

One friend, well actually not a good friend a faux friend, said, "Judilee, your head piece reminds me of that gal comedian who did the telephone skit— one ringy dingy…2 ringy dingys… (She meant Lilly Tomlin playing Ernestine the telephone operator).

WHATEVER!

Well, she was my faux friend.

But now my headpiece has a happy ending…In 2000, Gwen, my soon to be daughter-in-law "borrowed" my headpiece for her wedding to Greg.

Yes!!

Not to worry, it didn't look like the telephone operator's headset! We reshaped it into a beautiful head-band like headpiece and attached a veil. Gwen looked beautiful and I was so proud that Gwen wore my headpiece. Suky would have loved it!

Recently our granddaughters asked if they could wear my headpiece when they get married. So there Ernestine!!

The flowers were done by Tish Long. Tish used all shades of pink, lavender and white with lots of baby's breath. I like baby's breath, it's so fluffy yet elegant even all by itself. Tish made beautiful baskets for every window sill in the church.

Before our wedding, I had designated special friends to remove the baskets from the church window sills, then take the baskets to the reception and place them on each table. After the reception was over, my buddies were to each take their basket home to enjoy. Sorta' like a tribute to their wonderful love and friendship to me and my family. Hey, it was a big treat. Those fabulous big beautiful baskets were a splurge! Tish also filled the alter vases, which I donated to church the next day. Tish made Jen and Jodi's bouquets and of course all those baskets for the window sills. Tish created a vision for us. She did a fabulous job.

Now about an hour before our wedding, Tish and her assistant went to the church to check on all the flowers. Remember it was the hottest day of the year... When they opened the doors, they were hit with an odd strong stench –like bad BO? Farts? Rotten fish? They could not figure out where the awful smells were coming from.

Pee U.

STINK.O.

That is until Tish stuck her finger into a floral arrangements oasis (that green Styrofoam stuff you stick the flowers into) and discovered cheese had melted over the oasis. You'll never believe this, but someone had actually put Limburger cheese into every single arrangement – ah shucks, even the altar vases and the tall baby's breath aisle arrangements.

Limburger cheese, yep, it's that soft stinky cheese. Being such a hot day it melted quickly. Since Tish had no time to redo floral arrangements, she went to the store and bought cans of spray, perhaps cinnamon or lemon, and sprayed the carpets, seat cushions, and kneeling pads, to try to keep the stench down.

Years later we found out who did it. I'll tell you later but face to face!

Again years later, at a dinner party at the Cooper's Home in Wayne,

I was seated next to Tish Long's husband, I think his name was Walter. We were all telling stories and he said, "Tish should write a book about her wedding experiences…"

One story especially came to his mind, about a bride with a blended family where "someone put stinky cheese in all the flowers and it melted into every arrangement", blah blah…

I was blushing when I looked at Walter and said, "I was that bride!"

He damn near fell off his chair!

Then more recently, Tish mentioned that "your sweet mother called me after your wedding to ask if I used cheese as a preservative in my flowers". Tish added that her call was "the best story ever!"

Now towards the end of our reception, around midnight, it was still a hot and humid evening, and as we were walking by the pool, someone pushed us in. By the time the bride and groom were fished out of the pool, Mark Lichtenfeld was wearing my headpiece! I think you did it, Fenstermacher! Fess up.

Actually, it felt so refreshing in the pool. I was only worried about my Hunka-Hunka-Burning-Love Belt! And of course, my handsome new husband.

But, OH, WHAT A WEDDING!

Judilee C. Bennyhoff

After a "dip" in the pool, the culprits with the very wet bride and groom. Left to right; Don Fanelle, the groom, the bride, Jim Rein, John Carney, Jennifer Traynor and Mark Lichtenfeld wearing my head piece.

Gong Show Necklace

On one of my first dates with George, I think maybe I was wearing my gong show necklace. Oh Lord, maybe I wore it with a black, hot pink, wide horizontal striped top. I know I did. Oh, just the vision makes me cringe.

I like big necklaces—no necklace is too big for me. When I drove a Mercedes, a friend said, "Hey, Judilee, you could rip that hood ornament right off your Mercedes and wear it around your neck. That looks just like you."

OH, go pound sand!

But my favorite necklace was my big shiny gold round disc (the size of a small tea cup saucer), which was worn on a thick black cord.

It was hard for me to bend my neck but somehow I persevered. Besides that big hunky thing was comfortable. Well, sorta—hmmm, well maybe not so much.

Over time my necklace became legendary. (*Legendary; an admirable person about whom stories are told.*) That'd be my necklace and me. All the family referred to my garish bauble as my "gong show necklace", referring to the silly TV show which featured campy performers who, when the audience had enough of their silliness, a big brass gong was rung to signal they were done.

Left to right; Jim Kostrubanic, George Bennyhoff, John Orr, Dale Bennyhoff, Greg Traynor, Don Bennyhoff

See the picture of all those handsome dudes? That's your father there...Jimmy, George, John, Dale, Greg and Don. Notice what they're all wearing around their necks. Gong show necklaces. Oh, how fun. The picture was taken at my surprise 60th birthday party. Someone went to a lot of effort to cut out large round circles of cardboard , then cover them with gold tinsel-like-stuff and put them on a black cord. Was it you Jen? Jodi? Nicole? Gwen? Kristin? The boys wore headbands adorned with feathers too. Jimmy is wearing his headband and Don has his head band around his belt. (It's not what you think it is in the photo...)

Someone made me a huge crown encrusted with big hot pink jewels, and even a scepter (*Scepter; a wand held as an emblem of regal or imperial power)!* My scepter was outlined in hot pink fluffy feathers. Do you see George (Skipper) holding my scepter in the photo? He looks so handsome. He'll always be my king.

It was such a fun, festive, wonderful birthday party. Thank you all so very, very much. I love each and every one of you. I wonder what you will do for my 100th birthday party …

The Sailor Girl – Not!

"So captain, what do you want me to do with these lines?"
I know what I'd like to do with these lines!

We had a lotta', lotta' fun and a lot of laughs, BUT, if you want to go nowhere fast—try sailing—George loved it.

I did not.

At all.

Period.

The end.

We had a 35 foot Island Packet sailboat called TALISMAN. Talisman means magical charm— but not in my case. We kept her in Rock Hall, Maryland, and sailed the Chesapeake Bay area—well, when we were under sail—whenever we had some wind.

Hardly ever.

Cripes, you've got all those lines (ropes) all over the deck— like spaghetti.

The lines are everywhere and what line goes where? Oh geez, besides you are going nowhere fast for all that effort say 4 knots…that's slow.

Now think about this for just a moment… how do you suppose all that yummy food gets magically on board the boat? Well, so now I'll tell you.

Back at home, you buy your groceries at the grocery store. Then you bring them home and try to find room in your refrigerator for all your various items and treats. The next day, you repack and transfer all those groceries into coolers and tote bags, not paper bags – they rip – I know. Then lug everything to your car once again.

In a few hours you arrive at your marina. If you're lucky, you grab a metal cart or two, it looks like a wheelbarrow…then once again, you unpack your car, place groceries, booze, clothes, towels, sheets and books, sodas… blah, blah, blah.. into the carts.

Then you march along the long docks until you finally reach your boat, which is sitting in a slip (no, not a slip you wear but a boat slip *(slip; a space for a boat between two wharves or in a dock)*. Which reminds me, you pay rent to the marina to park your boat in that slip. You are charged by the foot. Bigger the boat – bigger the bucks. Thousands of dollars a year just to park the TALISMAN in her slip. To me it was like putting perfume on a pig! What a waste!

Now where was I?... talking about the carts...oh, yes, those damn carts were top-heavy and hard to push, too. May I remind you it could be 80 – 90 degrees. Hot.

Whew, I'm out of breath already.

Capt'n George saw me huffing and puffing and he helped me push my cart. As he should, he is the captain.

Hey are we having fun yet?

Not.

Well, we finally wheeled our way towards our boat, passing many boats with names like *Mom's Mink, Olive or Twist* (their dingy was *Gimlet*) and *Tuxedo* (a boat with a black hull and white deck). Then we finally reached the TALISMAN. We'd empty the carts by passing the bags over the lifelines. Finally, we're in the cockpit. Say, isn't that another funny word. Hallelujah! Already I'm exhausted and worn out. It's hot. And I'm a baby. (OK, I'll admit it, you know and I know that I am!)

You go through the companionway, go down six steps and you're smack in the galley (nautical term for kitchen). The "refrigerator" used to be an ice box with 2 or 3 blocks of ice for cooling. Try lugging those babies to the boat, eh. Now picture a large square hole cut out of Formica – with a lid. Ah, the "refrigerator". It's so damn deep, if I stretch my arm out, I can just barely touch the bottom of the refrigerator. My big feet almost leave the floor.

...Let's fast forward to lunchtime...

We have guests onboard, we are under sail – going a little fast – and it's getting to be lunchtime. Oh wonderful.

I'll go down below to the galley to prepare another gourmet lunch. I have the exact same menu each time we have guests onboard.

K.I.S.S. (keep it simple stupid) I'm no fool!

Picture this - the TALISMAN is healing-over (like leaning or tilting to one side) and I'm down below in the galley trying to make sandwiches.

Also, I'd like to refresh your memory that it's a hot, humid day – and even hotter below deck in my galley.

Alone.

If you're wondering why no one is down below helping me make lunch, there's really only room for one person.

That'd be me.

Now I'm soooo hot. I have a wet tea towel around my neck trying to keep cool. I'm sweating like a little piglet. Well, a piglet, forget the little.

Meanwhile, up on deck, Capt'n George is at the wheel, probably singing his sea chanteys and entertaining our guests.

Down below, today's sandwich-of-the- day was fresh turkey breast, Cooper sharp cheese, Jersey tomatoes and lettuce and mayonnaise. Ever read the label on the Hellman's mayonnaise jar? "Bring out the best" it says. Not in my case.

Wouldn't you know it, one wanted mustard, one wanted relish, and two with mayo. So I'm down there, way down in the ice box trying to find the condiments. My whole head's down in there still lookin' and rootin' and, once again, my feet left the floor.

And that's no B.S.

Well, at least I got cooled off for a few seconds. Hey, I could have been stuck down in that deep ice box. Feel for me here. Ah, I finally located the mayo, opened the lid, the jar slips, and now I have mayo all over the counter, including between my fingers. So heck, I just spread the bread with my fingers. No one would ever know.

After the turkey, next came the cheese. The Cooper sharp cheese was sliced so thin that it all stuck together like a cheese block. Ever had that happen? You know you did.

Then those luscious Jersey tomatoes – just try to cut one while listing over – the seeds flew everywhere. One good thing here, Capt'n George knew my culinary skills weren't the best so he made sure I had a dull knife for slicing or I'd be missing a finger.

I'm hot, still sporting the wet tea towel around my neck, mayo between my fingers, seeds everywhere.

Then I remembered the pickles. Sweet? Dill? Bread and Butter? I didn't ask – they got what they got – the pickle of my choice. And I wished I were pickled!

By then, hell, forget the lettuce and S&P. Yep, I made another little mess. A sticky gooey mess of pickle juice, seeds and mayo all over the counter top. Thanks heavens I was down below all alone in my kitchen, err, galley.

The sailor girl NOT.

By now I'm fighting for every inch of counter space to arrange the four plates with my gourmet sandwiches. Now this is the absolute truth. My tea towel fell from around my neck, hit one sandwich, which landed on the floor mayo side down.

Uh oh.

I just picked it up off the floor and plopped it on a plate. I always wondered who got that sandwich.

Eventually the plates were filled and I handed them up the companionway to our guests.

"Anyone for chips?"

"How about a nice cold drink?"

Bon appetite!!

Phew!!

P.S. I must confess the sailor girl has a boat now. Ah, yeah, really. It's a little (Ranger Tug) tugboat called JUBILEE. I wanted to name her Little Toot or Big Toot. But Capt'n George wasn't too thrilled with my idea for the name of our tug. His dislike for my suggestion was cemented when Greg called and said, "Benny, whatever you do, do not let Mom call your boat Little Toot." Oh, well, you win some and you lose some. Capt'n George named it JUBILEE (get it?) and I like that. I do like to go tootin' around the bay in our little tugboat with my wonderful captain. ☺

Captain George and Judilee on Jubilee

The Head

Hey, did you ever go to the bathroom on a boat?

If you say "No", lucky you.

The bathroom on a boat is called "The Head." The toilet looks like a toilet, but it doesn't flush like a toilet. Ours had a left-hand pump. Now pretend you're on a boat and you have to pee. Before you pee you must pump 4-5 times just to get water into the bowl.

Oh, and every so often you'd put 12 drops of Baby Oil (ole) into the bowl to lubricate it—so it pumps easier.

Then do your thing.

Wipe with 3 or 4 squares of 1- ply, then pump 5-8 times to "flush". We even had to have special marine toilet paper for our boat.

Good Luck.

Pump like mad and if you had a bowel movement, God help you! You just keep on-a-pumpin' until your arm hurts. And 'til your turd slowly, very slowly, disappears from sight. So where do you think all that pee and poop goes?

Judilee's Jubilee

Come on now; think about it—you're on a boat. Land ho' is not close by.

Well, your waste goes through a black hose into a holding tank! And when it gets full you go to a pumping station where you pay $5.00 for a pumpout of pee and poop.

The very first time I saw that pumpout procedure, I was speechless.

It's like pumping gas, only in reverse, and then out comes all that brown liquid.

Gross.

Yuck.

That's why I love sailing so much.

After a weekend of anchoring in quiet creeks and coves, never touching land, our holding tank's getting full. (Keep in mind we had guests, so there were four of us on board the *Talisman*.)

The cabin is slowly starting to have an odor.

Stink.

I hid lavender and lemon sachets in every nook and cranny but sometimes it just didn't help.

Pee U.

Our guests pretended not to notice the smells, but I know what they were thinking…your boat sure smells like shit.

Ah, yeah.

True.

It's tight quarters sleeping on a boat too. Capt'n George and first mate me, slept in the forward berth. The "head" is right next to our berth, say only 4-5 feet away from my head.

Only a door separated us.

Geez, I felt sorry for the sailor who had a gas problem but the melodic noises sure lulled me to sleep!

So here's to pleasant dreams!

NOT.

My Bestest Buddy

Susan and her best buddy

Susan Mader Brown was my bestest buddy. She was the sister I never had. Susan was bright, fun, pretty, stylish and on-the-go kind of gal. She had such panache. *(Panache; flair, grand manner.)* I loved her so much. We met at the Junior Saturday Club, a wonderful women's club in Wayne. I believe I was in my early thirties when we became friends.

A few years later, Susan became a widow.

I was a divorcee. (I never liked that word— there should be a softer kinder word for divorcee, don't you think?)

Ah, Susan and Judilee's perfect day together??

Lunch and shopping? Or shopping then lunch? Decisions, decisions. Now not to sound vain or materialistic but let's face it—we were vain and materialistic. And Susan was just about as bad as I was.

We weren't quite the Main Line snobs. Well almost. I take that back. No we were not snobs. Susan and I would have lunch at a lovely restaurant, we'd get invigorated with ice-tea—two lemons per glass. Then we'd hit every gift shoppe, boutique or book store from one end of the Main Line to the other.

Laughing and carrying on together— always chitchatting. Dressed to the 9's, we thought we were fashionistas! Susan and I appreciated culture and liked the finer things, i.e., Tchotchkes (what?!) that's a fancy-dancy word for knick knacks (junky trinkets.)

I vividly remember our purchases…

1. Pretty picture frames covered in gros-grain ribbon; Susan bought a green frame and I bought a blue frame.

2. Cachepot; *(cachepot* [kash-po]*: a decorative pot, jar especially for house plants)*. And we both liked white accessories and snapped them up at The Little House Shop at Spread Eagle Village.

3. We each bought black belts— Elvis like— but now mine's too small and darn it all!

4. We loved to stop at the Reader's Forum Book Shop in Wayne. The two owners were always so helpful in recommending just the right book for each of us.

5. Oh yes, off to Neiman Marcus (we laughingly called it,

"Needless Markup") at King of Prussia Mall… (My eyes still light up when it's in a Neiman Marcus shopping bag.)

6. Susan and I bought Chanel lipsticks. Color #55. We had such fun trying on all the lipstick shades and no doubt drove the sales lady nuts. Actually, the 3 of us had a good time together and the sales lady wanted to join us for lunch!

Susan and I usually had the exact same taste.

One time she called me from Vail, Colorado and told me she had just bought the most fabulous ski outfit. A black one-piece tuxedo with fur cuffs. And she bought it at GORSUCH in Vail Valley, no less. $Cha-ching-cha-ching$.

"Eat your heart out, Judilee."

Weeeell, meantime back in Pa., it just so happened, that George and I returned from Salter's Ski Shoppe where he bought me a bee-u-tee-ful ski suit.

Fabulous!

Now guess what it looked like?

Come on now…take a guess…

Give up?

It was a black tuxedo one-piece with fur cuffs. The <u>identical</u> ski outfit as Susan's.

But mine was on sale! I never ever told Susan my ski tuxedo was on sale— she was sooo happy and I'm not a Kilroy to burst her bubble.

I really wanted to tell her. In the worst way!

Speaking of ski suits, my dream was to one day ski the Matterhorn in the Swiss Alps—and my dream did come true. I had my picture taken in front of the Matterhorn wearing—what else—my black tuxedo one-piece ski suit…

Susan would be proud.

You know, I still have that ski tuxedo up in the third floor cedar closet and I just cannot part with it. Never, Ever. So you see Susan and I were always on the same page. Again. Anywhere.

But there was one thing that I did not like about Susan.

At all.

Her perfume. She always wore Carolina Herrera by Carolina Herrera. I thought she smelled like skunk cabbage! So much for her eau de parfum. I always wore 'Angel' by Thierry Mungler.

And Susan said, "Well, you're no angel in your Angel".

Humpph …

Then Susan got ALS (Lou Gehrig's disease). She gradually went from a cane, to a walker, to a push wheelchair, to a heavy-duty electric wheel chair.

Good Lord.

We're living in Pennsylvania with the 5 kids and Susan is now living in McLean, Va. and remarried to Jeffrey Brown—a great guy.

I'd hop in my car, drive to Susan's house and then hop right into bed with her. We'd spend our days and nights together enjoying each other. Susan and I would reminisce, I'd read to her, we'd watch movies, and laugh and eat. Oh, and drink wine…sometimes lots of wine.

Susan and I both loved to eat. Especially sea scallops and potatoes. We never met a potato we didn't like! For my last dinner with Susan, before heading home the next day, she talked to her Jamaican cook and requested fresh sea scallops and potatoes. Now we thought the cook understood Susan's request. (not so much!) We were sooo looking forward to our sea food extravaganza. When dinnertime came, I combed and fluffed Susan's hair, got her to the table, lit the candles and poured the wine (she could drink wine from a straw). We were so hungry...And...

Herrrre's dinner...oh how our eyes twinkled with anticipation.

Do you know what her Jamaican cook served us?

A big plate of...

SCALLOPED POTATOES!

Nuttin' else!

WHAAA. So we just laughed, and had more wine with our potatoes.

Every 4th of July weekend Susan and Jeff would join us sailing on the Chesapeake Bay.

We had a sailboat called *Talisman* and we kept her in Rock Hall, Maryland.

Towards 'the end' Susan was on a respirator.

One of her last wishes was to sail one more time on board *Talisman*.

Our destination was always St. Michaels, Maryland.

Now how on Earth are we going to get Susan on board?

But it just so happens that the boat, *Panacea*, right next to our boat slip, belonged to our good friends, Bob and Jeanne Honish. Bob's also our doctor so he'd help us find a way to get Susan on board.

Might I remind you it was a hot, humid, sunny summer day- in the 90's!

The boys, George, Jeff, and Bob rigged up a pulley system, attached it to the boom…cranked her up, lifting Susan right out of her wheelchair— her legs dangling—and put her right into a boson's chair. Then the boys hoisted and swung Susan over the finger dock, over the water, and slowly lowered her down the 6 steps right into the main salon in our boat.

Susan wore a big wide smile and she said, "Now this is what I call haulin' ass!"

And we all sailed into the sunset— all together again.

On one of my last visits to see Susan, we planned her funeral. She made me promise that when she goes to heaven, that I would do her makeup and her nails.

Oh, and not to worry, her Jamaican cook was great at styling her hair just the way she liked it—and she would do her hair.

Phew!

The cook wasn't too good in the kitchen…but I guess she's great with Susan's hair… (And as you now know, I am not a very good hairdresser!)

So I promised.

The day Susan died, her family called and said she would be ready tomorrow for me to do her nails and makeup.

Oh, by the way, her Jamaican cook had returned to Jamaica for a little holiday and could I please do Susan's hair?

OH MY GOD.

George and I drove to Virginia. To the funeral home.

Numb.

We were sitting upstairs in a small chapel-like setting when the funeral director came in and said he was ready for me now. Susan was downstairs waiting.

OH LORD.

I did ask the funeral director if he would position Susan in such a way that when I opened the door, I would see only the back of her head first. I needed time to see her and to adjust.

It took me a LOOONG, really LOOONG time until I collected myself, somewhat, got composed, somewhat, said my prayers and took deep deep breaths. And then slowly, one at a time, I walked down the stairs and opened that door knowing Susan was behind it.

And there she was, Susan, my bestest buddy, on the morgue table.

I cannot begin to articulate my emotions in seeing Susan on the cold morgue table.

I was utterly shattered, felt such deep sadness and also great pressure in my tasks ahead. Also, I had a time restriction as Susan's viewing would begin in just a few hours.

O.M.G.

As I stood over her, sobbing and thinking, how on Earth can I ever do this…the door slowly opened. And there he stood in the doorway—my wonderful husband George.

He said, "I thought maybe you could use a little help."

"Let's name our business 'Happy the Clown Makeup Company' and our first customer will be Susan. She'd love that." So we went to work together.

Susan was dressed in her pretty lace wedding dress—the one she wore when she married Jeff.

George tried putting on her large clip earrings. They kept falling behind her back. He tried at least 3 or 4 times and finally Susan's clip earrings stayed on. (Just because…)

He used hot rollers and had to hold them one at a time (just because…) George did a wonderful job as Susan's hair stylist.

Meanwhile, my makeup brushes were flying…aqua blue eye shadow, eyeliner, mascara, rouge and lipstick. Chanel. #55—the lipstick we bought together at Neiman Marcus.

But I did not spritz Susan with her Carolina Herrera perfume. No way.

Susan was coming to life and lookin' good, if we do say so ourselves.

Go "Happy the Clown Makeup Company"!

One thing that I do know for sure is…I'm a friend to the very end. And George is too.

Happy the Clown Makeup Company

Can you believe that exactly one week after Susan went to heaven, my brother Gary (then a funeral director in Lewisburg, Pa.) called us and said...

"Are you two still in business with your Happy the Clown Makeup Company?"

"Yes."

"I need you to bring your cosmetic bags and come up ASAP (as soon as possible) as Aunt Peggy has just died."

"OH NO. Oh no." I was sooo sad.

Aunt Peggy was my mother's sister and I adored her— well, I idolized her is more like it.

Here's a little bit of her essence. First off, Aunt Peggy was beautiful— her dark hair was worn in a Page Boy (i.e., long and turned under) she was thin and always so smartly dressed. When I was a little girl— say 9-10 years old— Aunt Peggy opened a dress shop in Lewisburg called "The Peggy Lee Shoppe."

Mother and I would often visit her dress shop and while those two chatted away, I'd look, well, root around in all of her belts—which Aunt Peggy displayed in large baskets. Sometimes I got the belts all twisted up. I'd try on lots of belts and then I'd parade around her shop— occasionally heckling the customers. Ok, I did.

Aunt Peggy lived at the back of her shop—and when they 'shooed' me back there, I'd play with her perfume bottles. Aunt Peggy wore Chanel. She had a collection of perfume bottles. Aunt Peggy said I could put "on a little spritz of Chanel— put a little dab behind each ear and on each wrist." "Just a little dab'll do it." Aunt Peggy had various perfume bottles—some bottles were so pretty—other bottles not so much.

But I especially liked the lavender glass bottle— it had a lilac cord and a squeeze-like bulb at the end of the cord. That particular lavender glass perfume bottle was called an atomizer: *(Atomizer; an apparatus for reducing liquids to a fine spray.)* Ah, a spray. I liked that lilac bottle. It was pretty.

Oh, I had such fun! I skipped around Aunt Peggy's room squeezing that lilac bulb at the end of her perfume bottle. I spritzed her lamp shades, pillow shams, vanity stool...

Well, then I decided I'd try on every scent myself. I put a dab behind my ears and on each wrist— just like Aunt Peggy suggested. I'd spritz my hair, behind my knees and all around my neck. I do remember my neck— I didn't like that application as my neck got moist, err wet, which made my dress wet around my neck. Ooh, I still vividly remember that—not a good memory.

Aunt Peggy's room became a cloud of many scents.

Pepe Le Pew comes to mind (isn't he a skunk?)

Well, they left me alone for sooo long— so what's a little girl to do?! But play—with all of Aunt Peggy's perfume bottles...

And speaking of Chanel, Aunt Peggy told me that one day, when I grew up, she would give me one of her prized Chanel bottles. I could hardly wait to grow up.

Well, maybe thirty years later, around Christmas time, Aunt Peggy gave me a beautifully wrapped present. She always had a knack for making her gifts look special— just the right wrapping paper, ribbons and bows— even her gift tags were unique. And you all know what was inside Aunt Peggy's present to me, don't you? You guessed right? When I opened the box— there it was— Aunt Peggy's Chanel perfume bottle. I'm so sentimental, that bottle is still on my shelf in my bathroom today. It still has a wee bit of perfume in the bottom—think I'll dab a little bit behind each ear and on each wrist. Just a little dab'll do it! After all, it is Chanel.

Unfortunately, I should get back to the Happy the Clown Makeup Company story.

When George and I arrived at the funeral home, I saw my beautiful Aunt Peggy in a casket—still looking smart and stylish. She was wearing white wool slacks and a grey cashmere turtleneck or were the colors reversed—a white cashmere turtleneck and grey wool slacks. I really don't remember but what I do remember is she wore an impressive big gold and silver broach (pin). I used to play with that pin in her Peggy Lee Shoppe.

After "The Happy the Clown Makeup Company" was finished getting Aunt Peggy "ready", her daughter, Pat, arrived at the funeral home to see her mother before the viewing began. She told us, "You know mother always wanted some nice boobs—can you do a little something for her in that department?"

"Hey, maybe I can fix that", said my brother Gary. He went right to his preparation room and returned to the parlor with a wad of cotton batting.

Then we all went to work together to enhance dear Aunt Peggy's figure. When we stepped away, we thought…hmmm maybe it's not just right.

So we went back to work and added bigger wisps of cotton and once again we stood back to admire our creativity and found her boobs way too big—like Dolly Parton's.

On our next try, out came some cotton. Now, Aunt Peggy's boobs were sorta' lopsided.

Down girls.

So once again— in with some cotton— out with some cotton, until, Ahhh, Aunt Peggy now looked just right!

When Pat returned to the parlor to view her mother, she said, "Oh my, mother would be so proud—and besides she'd simply love all that attention."

Once, again, Go Happy the Clown Makeup Company!

Ca-Ca-Claustrophobia

Claustrophobia; an abnormal fear of being in an enclosed or narrow place. Yep, that's what I have. Claustrophobia.

While living in New York City, in the 1960's, there was a black out and I got stuck in an elevator.

It was packed.

Going nowhere fast.

A large man, very large, was so beside himself that he actually lit up a cigar, which set off a chain reaction, which made a baby cry, and then set off some teenagers screaming "get me out, come and get me outa' here."

Well, my heart was racing so fast, I thought I'd croak in the corner of that elevator. Now I could embellish this story, but really, I don't exaggerate (hard to believe, isn't it?!) But we were all sealed and stuck in that dark elevator for about 10 or 15 minutes (but Lordy, it seemed like hours in there.)

I know what you're thinking; no, I did not pee my pants. I was a big girl wearing big girl panties.

Now fast forward—many years later, George and I were getting ready to go to Switzerland to ski with our ski group—the Ryans, Stuntebecks, Frenchs, and Somers. Now stay with me here and I'll try to tie this story together for you. Well, maybe so, maybe no, but I'll try.

One day, Dolly Somers, my good buddy, said to me…"Hey, Judilee, with your claustrophobia how will you ever be able to ride a gondola?" (*Gondola; a cabin suspended from a cable used especially to transport skiers*). "You know, in Europe that's the mode of transportation for skiers. Sometimes they use trams too."

"Uh Oh. Oh geez. Really."

So once again, I said to myself—"myself—I have a choice to either stay home and sulk or get help to go."… So I got help to go…

A wonderful psychologist helped me overcome my claustrophobia. I really wanted to go to Europe to ski— and besides I had a new black tuxedo ski suit. La dee dah for me. Now if I could only ski.

Last year as I was reading Time Magazine, there she was, my psychologist, being recognized for her excellence in treating post-traumatic stress disorders. Whoa, she's famous and she helped ME. She said the possibility of my being constricted (stuck) in a gondola, while skiing in Switzerland, are pretty remote. But if I was ever in that situation where I couldn't immediately remove myself—just remember 2 words…."SO VHAT" (SO WHAT. My psychologist has an accent.)

Also, the good doctor suggested deep breathing and keeping my mind occupied (now that's easy, as my mind sometimes is thinking about two things at once.) And the deep breathing—take a deep breathe, hold it for 5 seconds, release, and again for 10 or more times—I can do that. Piece-o-cake.

Now can you guess what happened to me when I was skiing in

Judilee's Jubilee

Switzerland, high over the Swiss Alps? Ah come on, give a little guess—humor me here. Hey, you guessed right…I DID get stuck in that gondola with Dolly and George, high over the Swiss Alps, swinging and swaying back and forth. And once again, I'm going nowhere fast.

SHIT.

Now this time I almost crapped my tuxedo…wouldn't you? Within seconds, I felt sheer panic, my mouth was like dry cotton—so what to do? I kept my pride and did not carry on like a nincompoop but I really wanted to scream like a Looney bird in the movie, "One Flew Over The Cuckoo's Nest."

What to do? What to do? Think Judilee. I immediately removed my lanyard, *(lanyard; string-like ID worn around ones neck)*, which held my ski pass. Then I started to tie knots, lots of little knots with my lanyard string. Ah yes, my deep breathing exercises. Breathe in-and-out, in-and-out, deep breathes. Come to think of it, I really did belong in "One Flew Over The Cuckoo's Nest" that with my deep breathing and tying little knots with my lanyard. I was very busy.

So there I am still stuck in the gondola, high above the Swiss Alps, still tying those little knots, and still breathing in and out, trying to keep my mind occupied (what I really wanted to do was bang my head against the glass surround of our gondola…) then finally, I just gave up and said "OH, SO VHAT"…

Ah, the Matterhorn, Switzerland. Left to right: Front row; Judilee, Mary Stuntebeck, Dolly Somers, Bob Somers; Back row; George, Jean French, Mike Ryan (behind Jean), Priscilla Ryan, Tom French, Clint Stuntebeck

Lob-stah (Lobster)

Miss Judy likes to eat, especially lobster. One time daddy took me to the Lewisburg Inn for their "Wednesday Night Lobster Special".

Mother wasn't that fond of lobster, and besides she had bridge club that night.

So there we were daddy and I sitting in a booth across from each other - pigging out on our lob-stah tails and baked potatoes oozing with butter and sour cream.

Now as I was about to take my very last bite of lobster…a teeny tiny red spider emerged from under that green lettuce-like garnish (what's that called anyway?)

When the nice waitress came to remove my plate, I told her about the cute little red spider, which was still on my plate scurrying around to get back under the lettuce leaf. The waitress freaked out and didn't like that little red spider. She told the manager and the manager told me that the Lewisburg Inn would happily give me a complimentary dinner and they were so sorry about the spider incident.

They hoped we'd come back again real soon.

ARE YOU KIDDIN' Absolutely.

Months later daddy called and said, "Come on up, honeygirl, and I'll take you back to the Lewisburg Inn for a nice lobster dinner. And, oh, don't forget to bring you bug box along!"

This year my son, Greg, sent me a wonderful birthday present, a Lobster Gram. It was a full lob-stah meal, clam 'chow-dah', butter, crackers – even a bib which I always need.

I was so excited and didn't even share much of my lobster dinner with George.

Now that wasn't nice of me, but, hey, don't judge me too harshly, I did give him the little bag of oyster crackers. He likes oyster crackers. (Ah, and you know I gave him a bite of my lob-stah…a very little bite.)

The Lobster Gram slogan is, "We make gourmet memories!" Ain't that the truth!?

Oh, my goodness, I almost forgot this recent dining experience.

George and I were "down the shore" and since it was our wedding anniversary, we went to a highly recommended, expensive restaurant in Margate. It was wonderful. Worth the wait.

George saw the full lobster dinner on the menu and said, "Hey, honey, it's our anniversary today. Why don't you get the whole lobster dinner?"

Splurge.

It took me 2 seconds to order the full lobstah dinner.

George had a chop.

Now you know, and I know you know what I'm about to tell you.

You're all onto me, with my very last bite of lobster I found a thin, silky black hair lying right across the lobstah-tail.

Honest. I have blonde hair.

Wellll, George looked at me and said, "Don't even think about it!"

Hey, what can I say—the owner comped my meal. She sent over a dessert tray with a candle on top of their signature blueberry pie to celebrate our anniversary…

Fabulous. Thank you – thank you.

We gave the waitress a big tip which paid for my dinner. George and I had a memorable anniversary dinner and I can hardly wait until my next lob-stah extravaganza.

P.S. You know I like to think daddy's looking down on me now and he sent that lob-stah dinner my way.

Bunny the Bunny

George and I were invited to Gregg and Mary Miller's home in Radnor for a poolside dinner party. Mary is such a fabulous gourmet cook. It's always a treat to taste her culinary creations. George gets "good eats" there.

As you all know, I am not a cook. No, not at all. I'm sorry about that (ah, not really) but I just don't get it in the kitchen, nor do I like to be in the kitchen. However, I do have a few fun aprons—one looks like I'm wearing a bikini top with boobs with a Hawaiian skirt. The other apron looks like I'm wearing a fancy dancy black dress. Oh, one looks like a Can Can dancer (like the apron in the picture with Daddy). Recently, Mackenzie returned from Spain and brought me a matador apron. Oh, I'll love that. Thanks, Mack. Even George has a fancy apron that looks like a tuxedo—as he should—because he now does most of the cooking (he doesn't call me Princess Judy for nothing.)

I do have 4 or 5 standby recipes and much to your surprise, I actually have a recipe or two in a cookbook.

Yes I do.

Judilee's Jubilee

You all probably think this is BS, but it's true. I have a few recipes in the Philadelphia Main Line Classic Cookbook.

Ok, check it out—page 205. It's called Chicken Pizzazz. It has 3 ingredients + water. Now that's my kind of recipe. Simple. I think Skipper's getting sick of that dish—so that's why he's now our chef.

Now where on earth was I going with this story? Aren't we at the Miller's for a poolside dinner party? Oh, that's where I was...let's go there...

Gregg Miller has a pet bunny called Bunny. She really is a he. He was a big dude for a rabbit. During cocktails in the garden, by the pool, Gregg got Bunny out of his crate and Bunny happily hopped around us munching on the green grass. Gregg's bunny, Bunny, was really cute.

And speaking of bunnies—since George and I have 19 grandchildren between us, people would say..."OH, YOU have 19 grandchildren—your kids are like rabbits." As John Orr once said, "We should change our last name from Bennyhoff to Bunnyhoff!" Hey, he should talk—he has five kids, three dogs, two turtles, and one fish.

Oh, that's funny, John. The Bunnyhoffs.

I asked Gregg (pestered him is more like it) if I could please hold Bunny. Meanwhile, back in the kitchen, Mary's probably like a one arm paperhanger. I'm no help – I'd rather hold bunny and shoot-the-shit outside, poolside, with a glass of wine.

So I'm back to buggin' Gregg...and he tactfully said, "You know, Judilee, Bunny really doesn't like to be held."

"Hmmm...oh, what a shame, Gregg. Just let me hold Bunny and see if he likes to be held. He just might be mesmerized by my ANGEL perfume. Can I hold him...please please..."

"Well OK, Judilee, you can hold him."

And Bunny liked me—he really did.

I remember what I was wearing that warm summer evening, sitting poolside in Gregg and Mary's beautiful backyard. I had on lime green capris and a brand new turquoise T-shirt, which was soft pima cotton…cha chink, cha chink…

We had a wonderful dinner and we were all happy—er, merry—and Bunny was happy too. Bunny was comfy, cozy and still sprawled out right between my boobs. Bunny's cold nose felt sooo good around my neck, especially on a humid summer evening. He just stayed there—right around my neckline moving gently back and forth. Bunny's nose felt sooo good and cool. Ahhh, yes.

Gregg said, "I'm just so surprised, Judilee, as Bunny usually doesn't like to be held but he seems to be so contented there with you."

HA-LOW. He <u>WAS</u> between my boobs. The male bunny rabbit that is; so what's not to like.

George and I returned home after another fun evening with the Millers. I was in our bedroom undressing and getting ready for bed, when I sensed that something was odd. Some damn thing was odd but I just couldn't figure it out—you kinda sorta know when something's not right but you still can't figure out what's not right. Ever have that happen? Well, I soon figured it out as Bunny had chewed the entire neckline, or the ribbing, off my new turquoise pima cotton T-shirt.

Just about that time, George came into our bedroom—I'm probably carrying on—and I showed him what had happened to my new turquoise pima cotton T-shirt. Ah, dang (I actually said Ah, shit) maybe I even said something stronger, because I like to swear. It makes me feel better. As I've gotten older, I really do like to curse. It relieves tension for me, sooo look out!

George just stood there and smiled and said, "You know, it could only happen to you, honey."

Well, at least I kept one guy happy that night—even if it was only a boy bunny wabbit, named Bunny.

Would You Believe— A Banana Pin?

I like pins too.

Recently I was in an antique shop (more like a junk shop) and I stumbled across a display of pins. All the various pins were displayed in an old revolving Timex watch display case. Remember those? The pins were going round 'n round in that old display case—like a Ferris Wheel only horizontally—going round 'n round and quite frankly looking at everything revolving made me dizzy and I'm already a dizzy blonde. I just couldn't keep up…

But lo' and behold— something caught my eye.

A BANANA PIN!

Ah ha!

Yes. Love at first sight.

This particular banana pin was made out of china. Now picture three bananas as a bunch— as a pin.

Cool and unusual, don't you think?

Judilee's Jubilee

Well, maybe not.

It spoke to me, so I had the saleslady walk all the way to the back of the shop to open the display case. She wasn't too thrilled to show me the pin. She wouldn't be caught dead wearing that banana pin, besides, she was kinda snooty. Ah, she wouldn't appreciate the banana bunch anyway.

Say, I was wonderin', why lock that Timex display case because everything revolving around in there was cheap and cheesy. The rhinestone pins were missing their sparkling stones—flower pins missing a petal…a dog pin missing his tail…

But I liked that banana pin.

Hey, would you wear that banana pin?

Be honest.

Probably not— that's why I got a deal here.

I bought that china banana pin and I put it on my sterling neck wire and that bunch of bananas hung happily 'round my neck.

I wore it with a big starched white shirt and paired it with a long yellow cardigan. Eat your heart out.

It was a hip-happening outfit, if I do say so myself.

And, I'll have you know— I did get a lot of compliments on my ensemble.

I don't wear earrings very much either.

Well, sometimes I do. Susan gave me her favorite earrings. Wearing her clip earring makes me happy, especially her big clips with the red, purple and orange stones.

My hair is long and straight and it covers up my ears, so you don't see my earrings.

Hey, guess when my ears grow they won't show either. I meant my ears. I'm told your ears grow when you get older.

That's good. I mean that my hair will cover my ears. Hey, I'm even confusing myself.

However, hold on just a minute here. I just thought of something.

Georgie Porgie is a lucky guy— no earring sales, no shoe sales, no necklace sales, either. I'm saving him a lot of moo-lah.

Maybe I'll wander into Wayne Jewelers or Farnan Jewelers in Wayne and look for a 'real' necklace…pin…hmm…a bracelet perhaps?

Sterling? 14-18 karat gold? Ou, now you're talkin.

NAH, probably not.

I'd much rather wear my Mercedes, or Gong Show necklace— or even the banana bunch around my neck. Or, on second thought… maybe I can accessorize my yellow banana pin necklace with those yellow clown shoes? Now, that'd be the cat's meow.

Miss Manners

Recently, a granddaughter (who shall remain nameless) didn't know how to set our table for dinner. "Doodie, where does the fork go—on the right or on left of the plate?" Ah ha, here was the perfect opportunity to give an impromptu etiquette lesson. *(Etiquette: conventional requirements as to social behavior).*

I was once a teacher at Patricia Stevens Finishing School in Philadelphia. I took a course at the school and was certified by the state of Pennsylvania to teach classes at the finishing school. I especially enjoyed teaching modeling and poise classes (although, I'm so klutzy and most certainly not too poised myself). But, I REALLY loved teaching etiquette (manners) classes. I soon realized that many students—mostly teenagers—lacked self-confidence and really didn't know right from wrong, so to speak, when it came to manners, nor did they have any idea what to do. At all actually…I was dumbfounded.

So here's a little guide that might help you thru life….

1. For a properly set table: the knife (blade in) and spoon is to the right of plate. Napkin and forks to the left of plate. Bread plate above the fork. Water, wine glasses go above the knife.

2. Never ever put your elbows on the table while eating, or chew with your mouth open. No exceptions here.

3. Place your napkin on your lap with the fold side out (towards the center of the table) and the 'ends' toward you. DO NOT use your napkin to blow your nose, wipe sweat from your head or clean your glasses. When you leave the table to go to the restroom or perhaps step outside to take a call, place your napkin on your chair. When your meal is finished and you are ready to leave your table, place your folded napkin to the left of your plate. Oh geez, one of my darling grandchildren balled up his/her napkin and put it on his/her dirty plate. I almost croaked. Don't worry, I'll never tell.

4. When a slice of lemon is served in your water, ice tea or Coke… immediately place your lemon into your glass. Hey, you don't want that lemon poking your nose as you're taking a drink do you.

5. Ah, the bread plate—my pet peeve—break your roll or bread in half before you butter. And when the butter is served on a butter plate, take your knife and place a pat of butter on *your* plate. DO NOT take butter from the butter dish directly to your roll or bread. I've seen people take a big fat roll and slather it with butter right off the butter plate. That is a NO NO.

6. When you're served soup or dessert in a bowl with a saucer underneath—and you're finished—place your spoon on the saucer. If you DO NOT have a saucer, then it's permissible to place your spoon in your bowl.

7. I'm sure you don't "double-dip", i.e., put your carrot stick into a dip—eat the end off—then put the carrot right back into the dip. I'm sure you all know not to "double-dip"…er, don't you…

8. Handshake: When you shake hands with someone—make it firm (not like you're shaking a wet worm) keep your wrist straight and always look the person in the eye.

9. Now when you get older and can have some wine, these simple tips might help.

If you are drinking white wine in a stem wine glass always hold it by the stem. White wine should be refrigerated and is always served cold. When at a restaurant, your bottle of white wine might be placed in a wine bucket filled with ice. (That's nice—and I'm getting tired of writing this—I could go for a glass of wine just about now myself…)

If you are drinking red wine—it is served in a wine glass with a larger 'bowl' (or bigger glass). Red wine is not refrigerated. Hold your red wine glass with your hand under the 'bowl' of the glass—your hand will keep your red wine warm. Cheers!!

10. For you grandsons, please put the toilet seat down. Thank you.

P.S. And behave yourself!

VR-O-O-O-M

My handsome husband, George (Skipper to you), is a car fanatic. Really, but you already all know that. Skipper can tell you the make and year of almost any car. And he's usually right on.

He dreamed of owning a Porsche again someday. A 911 Porsche. (Pronounced Porsh-AH) Skipper gets all excited when his monthly car magazines arrive, i.e., Car and Driver, Classic Cars and Sports and Exotic Cars.

It's a happy day for him.

Well, remember I had my interior design 'bid-ness' (business)? I scrimped and saved, on the sneak for about 9 ½ years and when his big birthday arrived…Guess what?

I surprised him with a Porsche. A 911. Carrera. Guards' Red.

He is one cool dude behind the wheel. George still drives his red Porsche around town. Honk when you see a red streak!

George even has driving shoes, black and yellow with bright yellow laces—now those shoes are cool—so maybe I'll borrow them sometime. He said they'd be too small for me!

Judilee's Jubilee

And he can blow that into his handkerchief!!

A couple years later, at Christmas time, his gift from me was to go to Birmingham, Alabama and attend the Porsche Driving Experience. YA hoo! The experience was to race Porches on a Grand-Prix race track, the real deal. Not an oval or stock car race track but a 2.6 mile track with 17 turns or in racing lingo, "twisties". I asked George to describe the Porsche Driving Experience and he said, "It was an experience of a lifetime. Porsches handle fast, are glued to the track—and sound G-R-E-A-T."

This might sound a little a naughty, but George uses the term, "slow in – fast out". He learned that when racing Porsches, you slow into turns and accelerate through and out of turns. When George was being rushed to emergency surgery, the nurses sure thought it was naughty when he kept shouting to Dale as we sped down the halls of the hospital... "remember Dale, slow in – fast out."

I was just thinking, you know his love of Porsches rubbed off on our kids...Jodi drives a speed yellow one, Dale has an '83 Porsche, at last count Jim Kostrubanic has two of them and Sophie's dream car is a Barbie hot pink Porsche Boxster. Let's face it... other members of the family have Skipper's car gene and lust after Porsches—hopefully, someday, their dreams will come true. My good friend, Ginny Riley, drove a white 944 Porsche. She looked cool in her car. Another good friend, Skip McClennen, drives a Porsche. He looks cool, too. Unfortunately for me—and fortunate for George—I can't even get the damn Porsche out of the garage. Too much power for moi.

George keeps his red Porsche immaculate and maybe he even rubs and kisses it. Do you think he does?

I think he does. I know he does. I saw him recently stroking and patting his red Porsche. I really did.

Hey, that's OK, honey; you just keep on kissing the car. And stroking it too!

VR-O-O-O-M....

George and his Porsche. He calls it "Sir Scarlet".

The Incredible Shrinking Doodie

Speaking of getting older, I'm much shorter now, too. I probably stand around five foot-four and that's with my shoulders erect like a soldier, stomach sucked in and my head reaching for the stars. And that's stretching it, too.

When I did a little modeling, I was, uh, about five-six and a quarter inches tall. You can figure out the math. Losing a few inches are we? Where the hell did it go? Somebody tell me. Please. I'm feeling so good but I'm getting sooo short. I now shop in the Petite department.

George is six-two with eyes of blue. He kids me about getting shorter. (I didn't say smaller, I said shorter.) Georgie Porgie said, "Hey Doodie, maybe by the time you're ninety you'll come to just above my waist."

Hummph! Oh, very funny.

So here's Skipper's suggestion. You all know he enjoys simple carpentry projects—he just finished making cellar doors for the outside of our 100 year-old home. He said making the cellar doors was a cinch. Hmmm, actually took him forever. He had a hell (sorry, heck) of a time removing the bolts from those old black strap hinges that adorn our cellar doors. (But don't tell him I said so.)

Now back to his secret special project for me. Skipper said he'd be happy to build me a special door. An in-and-out or come-and-go door. Just for me. Oh, how nice. Are you following? I realize it's hard to follow along here with this nonsense! Skipper said he'd do his best and make me a nice efficient door. The new door would have a large flap at the bottom. Perhaps the flap could be made of pliable rubber.

Do you know what kind of door he was referring to? It'd be like a large doggie door—only he'll call it a DOODIE DOOR.

Ahhh, that's a clever idea, Honey, thanks—but gee, no thanks. Maybe next year!

She Sees Sea Shells Down By the Sunny Sea Shore

Now try and say that fast. Three times. Oh, go ahead try it. Awe, come on you can do it. Try again. Oh, that was good.

Don't you just love sea shells? I bet that every single one of you, at some time or another, has bent down and picked up a pretty shell.

My good friend, Mary Page, is my shell idol. Mary is so well known for creating Sailor's Valentines. No, not the paper heart valentines you make for Valentine's Day, but the sea shell Sailors' Valentines. This describes them…

History of Sailors' Valentines

Folklore romantically portrays Sailors' Valentines as the work of homesick sailors passing time while on long sea voyages brought home to sweethearts at the end of their journeys. Though some have been the work of sailors, this beautiful shell art were, in fact, made by craftsmen in Barbados between 1830 and 1880. They were purchased by American and British sailors at this port of call and brought as souvenirs. Sailors' Valentines were made in octagonal wooden boxes. They were created with tiny shells glued in patterns on a cotton backing. Patterns include flowers, hearts, stars, and often included sentimental messages.

Mary was coauthor of a book on Sailor's Valentines called *Sailors' Valentines—Their Journey Through Time*. She's famous. And I wanted to make one. Once again, I probably heckled her (yes I did) until Mary said, "Why don't you come down, Judilee, and we'll make a Sailors' Valentine together?"

"Hallelujah. How about tomorrow?"

In a few weeks, there I sat, right next to Mary Page, in her Bryn Mawr home, downstairs in her shell room, playing with sea shells. I was in heaven.

Hmmm, now what to create? Mary gave me an octagonal box (8 sided) and a big baggie filled with assorted colored shells; green shells, purple shells, and blue shells—the colors reminded me of the ocean. Oooo, yes, I think I'll try to create a mermaid from the assortment of colored shells.

But doggone it, I just couldn't figure out what shells to use for my mermaid's hair. BINGO. I hatched an idea…I think I have an old branch coral necklace in my jewelry drawer, hey, maybe that'll work for my mermaid's hair. So I got my little nose scissors and cut my old branch coral necklace apart then gave my mermaid some hair. Red hair. Then I named her "Mary the Mermaid" after Mary S. Page. (I always wondered if she was thrilled or embarrassed with her namesake.)

We learned that the Sanibel Shell Show, in Sanibel, Florida is the most prestigious shell show in The United States. People enter the Sanibel Shell Show from all over The United States, Canada, Europe, and Asia hoping to win a "ribbon." 1st place ribbon (and always the coveted ribbon) is awarded a blue—2nd place is red—3rd place is yellow and Honorable Mention is green. Gee whiz, now wouldn't it be fun to go to Sanibel to see the famous shell show and perhaps go shelling on their fabulous beaches—after all, it is the shell capital of the world (wurd).

George had an idea, "I'll drive you down to Florida, sweetheart. Let's have another adventure, we'll stop and see Mary Jo and Steve Jefferson's in North Carolina. We love spending time with Steve and Mary Jo and enjoying their Southern hospitality. (Besides, Mary Jo is such a fantastic cook.) Then it's – Sanibel or bust!" And we did. And as always, we laughed a lot and had a great time together.

Can you believe I had the nerve to enter my "Mary the Mermaid" with my rinky-dinky shells. My colored shells were not like the beautiful expensive shells most exhibitors used. My category was: "Single Sailor's Valentine" hobbyist category. The judging was done in the evening, and the next morning, George and I went to see the shell show.

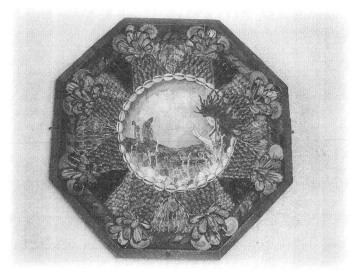

Mary the Mermaid

OH. MY. GOODNESS.

Sitting right in front of my "Mary the Mermaid" entry was a blue ribbon AND the Special Judge's Award for "Best Single Sailors' Valentine" hobbyist category.

George and I were flabbergasted. Dumb Struck. Oh Lordy, my halo popped up and twirled around a few times—but not for long.

As I walked up and down the aisles admiring exhibitor's work, I stopped in front of a beautiful, large, oval mirror entry, obviously covered in shells. I talked to the lady exhibitor and told her how much I liked her entry. Her mirror was clever and unique. And she said to me, "did you see that mermaid entry that everybody's talkin' about?"

"Ahhh..."

"Well, we in the shell community have never heard of her. I'm told she's from Pennsylvania and she marched down here and took a 'blue' (ribbon) and the Judge's Trophy for that mermaid of hers."

"Oh, is that so..." said I.

"And furthermore, did you see her mermaid's hair. I'm told her hair is from an old necklace she cut apart, and who ever saw a mermaid with red hair. And the exhibitor even has a funny first name."

At that point, I said, "Ahhh, wellll, ahhh, it was nice talkin' to you (not). I think my husband's lookin' for me..."

You know what, now that I'm telling my true tale, I must fess up and tell you that at the same time I entered "Mary the Mermaid" I also entered another shell work under the 'mosaic' category. Here's how that creation came to life.

About a year before, when I was visiting mother in her home, she looked so pretty sitting on her blue linen sofa in front of her bay window. Family pictures, orchids and hydrangeas were sprinkled across mother's window sill. To me it was such a warm homey sight, like home sweet home. I told mother, "You know, somehow I'm going to try to capture your family room in shells." Mother replied with a smile, "Oh, that'd be so nice, sweetie, I'm sure you will enjoy doing your shell work."

But I didn't have an octagonal box to use so, with coupon in hand, I bought a white square shadow box, and I was in 'bidness'. Hmmm, now what to call what I do as it's not a Sailors' Valentine because, obviously my box wasn't octagonal (8 sided). A friend suggested, "Judilee, why don't you call your shell work "Shellscapes" like in landscapes and seascapes. Oh, great idea, thanks John.

I was in my glory covering a blank canvas with shells. I work with teeny tiny shells, say smaller than my fingernails. Mussel shells became mother's sofa, white tusk shells transformed into her tieback curtains, sea urchin spines became her hardwood floor and sisal rug, apple blossom shells bloomed into her orchids and so on and so on...

Geez Louise, your family room is coming to life if I do say so myself. I will name my first shellscape after you and I will call it "Mother's Family Room" in honor of you.

George even made up a cute little ditty, which I placed underneath my shellscape.

Mother's Family Room

My ninety-two year old mother lives in a cute little house on the top of a hill. She loves watching the birds out her window, especially the cardinals which frequent her bird feeder. She enjoys her orchids and hydrangeas but mostly loves to be surrounded by pictures of her loving family.

Now back to the Sanibel Shell Show...

People seemed to enjoy "Mother's Family Room", especially the judge, Hannah Milman, one of Martha Stewart's editors. Hannah told me that mother's curtains so reminded her of her grandmother's ruffled curtains. That made me feel so good.

Holy Cow.

There, hanging on the wall above "Mother's Family Room", was a blue ribbon AND the special Judge's Award for "Best Picture or Mosaic. Hobbyist."

I hate to say this again, but not in my wildest dreams....

Mother's Family Room

I've had fun feedback on my new art concept "Shellscapes" and it seems to be enjoyed by people of all ages. So I'm still doin' it, well, that is after I finish this memoir. I was even asked to speak at a church group, St. John's Presbyterian Church in Devon, where they have monthly speakers. It was like taking show-and-tell to church. Gosh, it was fun.

This might be one of my last chapters, and I can't wait to play with shells again. I'm imagining maybe a Bake Shoppe or a Candy Shoppe—can't you just see the display case filled with pies, tarts, and cakes maybe lollipops.

Hmmm...or maybe a flower market with roses, tulips, hydrangeas.... oh, I can hardly wait! Stay tuned...

The End

(well, not quite….)

Made in the USA
Lexington, KY
03 May 2013